Offensive Football Systems

Keegan Dresow

If you have any questions, comments, suggestions, or if you want to discuss the book, I'd love to hear from you. Please email me at: keegan.dresow@gmail.com

All rights reserved. This book or any portion thereof may not be reproduced or used in any manner without the express written permission of the author.

Table of Contents

Introduction and Key 5
Single Wing 6
T Formation 10
Full House T Formation... 14
Split T 18
Wing T 22
I formation (traditional/non-option based) 26
I formation (option based) 31
Power I.. 35
Split back veer 39
Wishbone 44
Flexbone 48
Double Wing.. 52
Sid Gillman Offense 56
Vertical Offense (Al Davis)... 60
Air Coryell 64
West Coast Offense 68
One back 73
LaVell Edwards BYU Passing Offense 77
Air Raid 81
Run and Shoot... 86
Spread offense 92

Hurry up spread 97
Pistol Offense...103
Multiple..108
"Matchup" Offense 112
"Pro" Offense...116

Introduction

This book is intended to give a brief overview of the popular offenses of American Football. It is written not only to provide insight into popular strategies and schemes, but also as a brief guide for coaches who are choosing an offense to implement.

Football fans - and coaches in particular - are passionate about their scheme of choice. The beauty of football is limitless strategic possibility. The goal of this book is brevity. Nuances are missing, by design.

Key

- ● Offensive player
- ⬠ Defensive player
- ○ Possible ball carrier or possible pass receiver
- ⬟ Defender to be optioned
- ∿∿ Pre Snap Motion

Single Wing

Basic alignment:

Various alignments, but the ball is always "shotgun" snapped. There is a wingback, and lines are unbalanced. The quarterback is typically a shallow blocking back who is offset "a quarter of the way back." The ball is often snapped to the fullback (a back who is "the full way back") or a tailback at even depth or deeper than the fullback. The traditional single wing has no wide receiver; the eligible receivers are the weak tackle, the end man on the strong side, and the backs.

Brief description:

The dominant offense in the early years of football, the single wing still enjoys great success where executed properly. It is a running offense that employs misdirection and force at the point of attack. Once a staple at all levels of football, the single wing has faded from the game. Now, it is most popular at the youth level and retains some vitality at the high school level. It has achieved a small resurgence with the promulgation of the "Wildcat" offense, which borrows elements from the single wing.

Good for:

Teams that don't have a true quarterback can thrive with the single wing. The offense functions well with the type of athletes that almost all schools have: tough, midsized kids with decent athleticism. The backfield positions are interchangeable, and the success of the offense is not predicated on having a single dominant player.

Although the offense can be complex, it can be simplified for youth teams. With power and misdirection in the running game, it is a youth favorite.

The offensive line should be faster than they are big.

Bad for:

Teams that wish to feature a traditional quarterback or passing game should look elsewhere.

The traditional single wing does not feature wide receivers. It is not a "modern" offense and therefore will not make all players happy.

Advantages:

A ball control offense that does not require great athletes, the single wing can close talent gaps and keep a vulnerable defense off the field. The misdirection leads to big plays in the run game, and will frustrate opposing defenders.

Will give your team a strong identity.

Overwhelms the defense with numbers at the point of attack.

In theory, single wing principles can be applied to shotgun/spread formations and passing schemes, creating a more balanced attack.

Drawbacks:

The single wing is run heavy, without the ability to make up a deficit quickly.

Players who want to catch and throw the ball won't be happy.

Where it will work:

High school and youth teams; perhaps small college teams that fully commit.

Where it won't work:

Major college football and the NFL (except for elements of the spread/single wing "wildcat" hybrid).

Defenses that it will beat:

A soft or undisciplined defensive front will get eaten up by the single wing!

Defenses that it will struggle against:

A disciplined run stopping defense will have a good chance to beat a single wing team.

Final Word:

The single wing is a beautiful offense when executed well. With a variety of fakes and power runs, the defense will struggle to find the ball and be met with a wall of blockers when it does. The simple versions of the offense are perfect for youth play because they are powerful in the run game and easy to understand. However, the offense is one dimensional, making it ill suited for higher levels of play. It can be successful and explosive, but it takes a complete commitment and expertise. With fewer and fewer single wing gurus left, that expertise is hard to come by.

Spin Keep

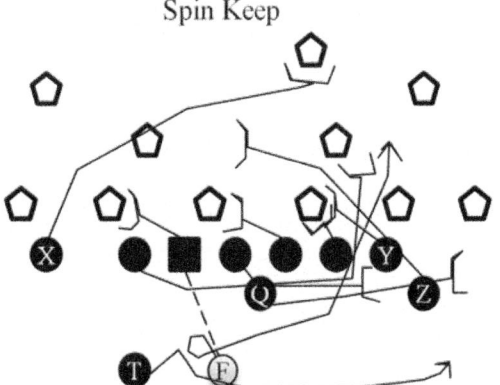

Theme: Spin fake provides deception; blocking uses angles and numbers

Spin Give

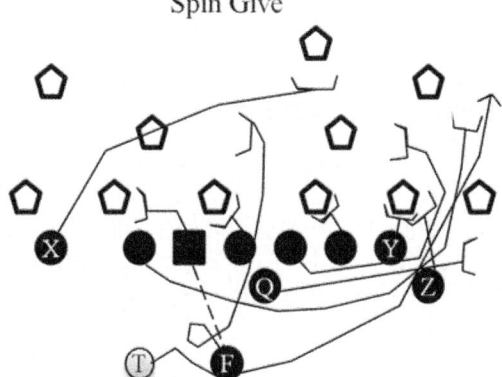

Theme: Spin handoff; deception and power at the point of attack

Give to Quarterback

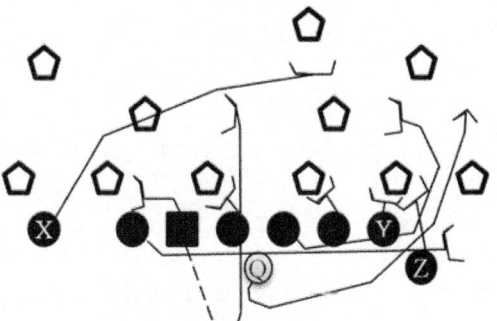

Theme: Snap to fullback, who hands to spinning QB; more deception and power

T Formation

Basic alignment:

Quarterback under center, three running backs in a row in the backfield (forming a T, along with the quarterback), often with two tight ends.

Brief description:

The T was one of the first football formations, dating to the late 19th century, before it was replaced by the single wing. The single wing remained the dominant offense in football until George Halas's Chicago Bears used the T to win the 1940 NFL championship 73-0 over the Washington Redskins. With the quarterback under center, the running backs could hit the line of scrimmage at full speed with power and precision. Halas used motion to spread the defense and either throw to the motioning back or remove a defender from the box to better run the ball. The formation allows the power of two lead blocking backs, or the deception of fakes to multiple players. Play action passes compliment the running game.

Good for:

The T formation requires a quarterback who is a great ball handler and good athlete. Agile, pulling linemen are also a necessity.

The power and misdirection in the run game rely on execution over talent, making the T a good equalizer for teams with limited talent.

Bad for:

The offense is complex, so it is not suited for young players.

If you want a modern passing game and have the players for it, look elsewhere.

Advantages:

Controls the ball with power and deception. Will help prevent fatigue if your roster is thin.

An equalizing offense for teams with limited talent.

Doesn't require great size or speed.

Top notch misdirection.

Drawbacks:

Resources on the historical T formation are slim.

The offense is complex and will fail without good execution. The timing and deception of the running game takes time, and you can't dabble with other offenses if you plan on installing the classic T formation.

No traditional drop back passing game.

Where it will work:

Youth, high school, and small college.

Where it won't work:

The NFL and major college football.

Defenses that it will beat:

Undisciplined defenses and defenses that can't stop the run.

Defenses that it will struggle against:

Disciplined, run stopping defenses will give the T fits.

Final Word:

The father of modern offense, the T formation brought the quarterback under center and introduced a quick hitting, deceptive offense to the game. It forced defenses to defend areas of the field that the single wing rarely threatened, and became THE offense during the mid 20th century.

Almost all modern offenses descend from the T, but it would be difficult to replicate the pure Chicago Bears T of the 1940s. George Halas created a complex scheme with varied motions and an intricate run game. A team that installs the classic T will need to commit to it over the long term. If they do, they'll have a powerful running attack, with as much deception as any offense, and a play action game to keep the defense honest.

Bears T Belly

Theme: Powerful play can be blocked variety of ways; also set up much deception

Bears T Outside Counter

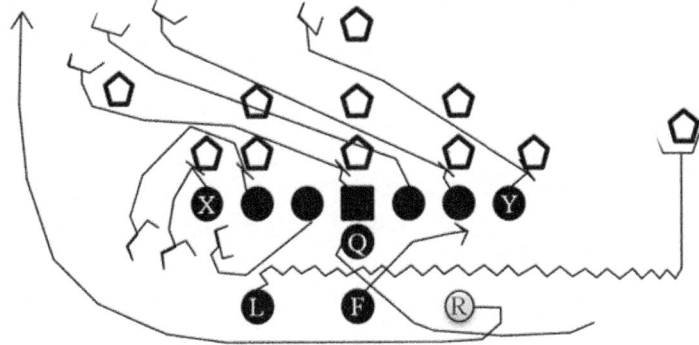

Theme: Fake to FB, loads of downfield blocking; "gadget" deception that fueled T

Bears T Play Action Pass

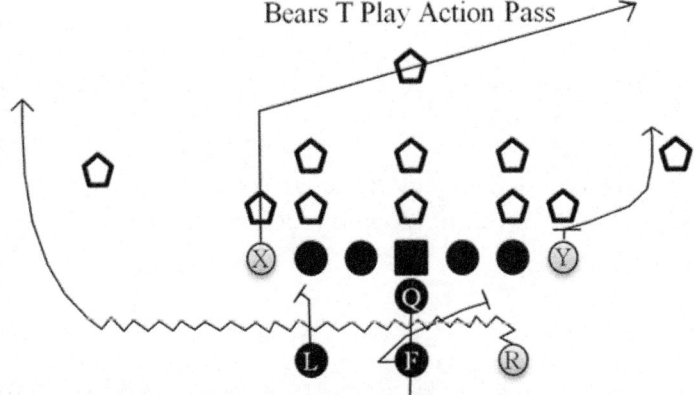

Theme: Motion spread field and backs gave run action while Bears attacked deep

Full House T Formation

Basic alignment:

Tight line splits, two tight ends, quarterback under center, and three running in a row in the backfield (forming a T, along with the quarterback).

Brief description:

The full house T is a brawling, rugby scrum of an offense predicated on power and misdirection in the run game. Few plays need to be installed, making it a youth favorite. It relies on fundamentals and discipline, and finds success at the youth and high school level.

Good for:

If you want a run first, run second, and run third offense, this is a great choice. A quarterback with good ball handling skills is a plus.

You don't need amazing athletes to have success with the full house T.

As a ball control offense, this is good scheme to prevent fatigue on a small roster.

Bad for:

Teams that want balance should look elsewhere. If you have a throwing quarterback, or multiple wide receivers to utilize, this is not the offense for you.

Advantages:

Ball control.

You won't have many turnovers.

Power.

Deception.

Simplicity.

Can keep a team with inferior talent in many games.

<u>Drawbacks</u>:

Predictable. The defense knows you are running.

Difficult to come from behind with this offense.

No pass balance.

Won't take advantage of wide receivers or throwing quarterbacks.

Not a big play running offense.

<u>Where it will work</u>:

Youth, high school, and perhaps at the small college level.

<u>Where it won't work</u>:

The NFL and major college football.

<u>Defenses that it will beat</u>:

Defenses that can't stop the run, or who chase fakes, will die against the full house T.

<u>Defenses that it will struggle against</u>:

Disciplined defenses that can stop the run.

Final Word:

The full house T is a powerful, deceptive running offense. When executed well, on one play the defense will be chasing the ball in three different directions, and on the next play they'll be overwhelmed with numbers at the point of attack. It doesn't take great talent to have success in the offense - good fundamentals, hard running, and a smooth quarterback will make it work. It doesn't have to be complicated, making it a youth favorite. If you are a youth coach who wants a simple and effective offense, or a high school coach who has a talent disadvantage or who wants to establish an identity of pounding the rock without mercy, this could be the offense for you. If you want balance, look elsewhere.

FB Trap

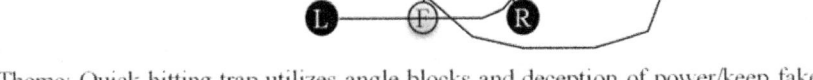

Theme: Quick hitting trap utilizes angle blocks and deception of power/keep fake

HB Power

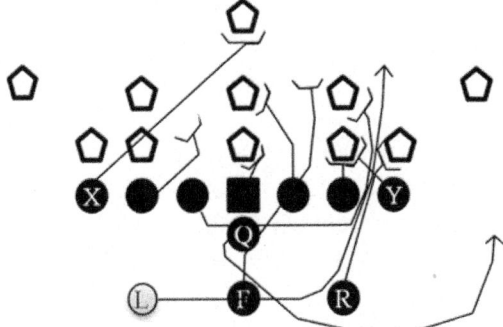

Theme: Back action and guard pull looks like Trap; power and deception

QB Keep (fake Trap, fake Power)

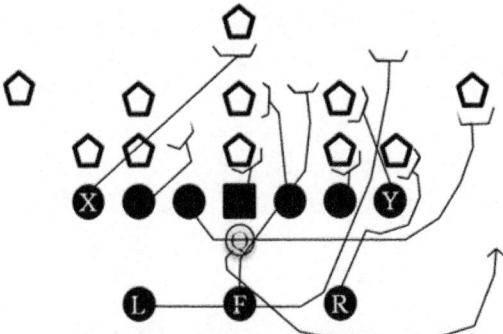

Theme: Same look as Trap and Power; displays the deception of the Power T

Split T

<u>Basic alignment</u>:

A full house backfield (like the T and full house T), but with wide line splits. Two tight ends or one tight end and one split receiver.

<u>Brief description</u>:

Developed by Missouri's Don Faurot in the early 1940s, the origins of option football are with the split T. By using wide line splits, the split T spread the defense more than the typical offense of the day. Rather than block all of the defensive linemen on a given run play, Faurot left one or two defensive linemen unblocked as option keys. This allowed his offensive linemen to block downfield. As for the unblocked linemen, the quarterback gave the ball (for example) if the defensive tackle didn't crash down, kept it if he did crash down, ran the ball if the end went with the pitch man, or pitched the ball if the end tried to tackle him. A former Missouri basketball captain, Faurot's goal was to create a basketball 3 on 2 or 2 on 1. It also meant that his linemen didn't have to defeat good defensive linemen in one on one battles. This idea revolutionized football and signaled the dawning of the option era in college football. Notably, Bud Wilkinson used the split T at Oklahoma to win a record 47 straight games - a record that still stands.

The option has become the prime threat for numerous top offenses over the years, from the veer to the wishbone to the flexbone to the I formation option to the spread option offenses of today.

In addition to the option play, the split T incorporated a number of quick hitting and powerful run plays, as well as a complimentary pass game, featuring halfback run/pass options as a staple.

<u>Good for</u>:

If you don't have a great throwing quarterback, the split T is an option. The quarterback does not need to be big or fast, but he does need to be smart and competitive.

Because you aren't blocking the defensive linemen on every play, this is a great offense for a team without road graders on the line. Quickness, discipline, and toughness are more important than brute force.

You can control the ball and win games in this offense without as much talent as your competition.

Bad for:

If you want to throw the ball with a modern passing game, this is not a good offense for you. It won't make wide receivers happy. If you have prototypical talent and a line that can win one on one matchups, you might look elsewhere.

Advantages:

Ball control run offense. The downfield blocking of the split T option makes this a big play offense.

It doesn't take amazing athletes to make this offense go.

You'll establish a strong running identity.

A simple offense that young players can understand.

Drawbacks:

Not a balanced offense. If you practice the option enough, you won't have time for a complete modern passing game.

Fumbles are a threat in the option game.

Won't keep quarterbacks and receivers who want a modern passing game happy.

Your defense won't practice much against passing; this will hurt if you play against spread teams.

Where it will work:

Youth, high school, and possibly small college.

Where it won't work:

The NFL and major college football.

Defenses that it will beat:

Defenses that can't stop the run will get beaten by the power runs and quick hitters.

Overaggressive defenses will give up big plays against the option.

Defenses that it will struggle against:

A fast, run defending front will cause troubles. Defensive linemen and linebackers who are fast and disciplined enough to take away one option and still play the next give the option fits.

Final Word:

The split T is the father of option football. It is old school big play football; combining a traditional churning run game with the high scoring option scheme. While the split T is rarely used today, it should be considered as a contrarian approach for teams that don't have talent suited for today's spread offenses. If you fully commit to this offense, you'll have the ability to run with power, misdirection, and the triple option. Your team can succeed because of execution, rather than pure talent. By controlling the clock you'll keep your defense fresh, an added bonus for thin teams. Not everyone will be happy with the run first approach, but this is not an offense that was ever truly stopped. It simply evolved into other forms.

Quarterback Option

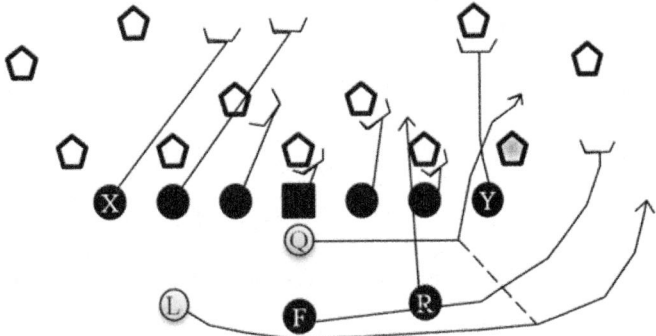

Theme: Forerunner to veer faked dive, optioned DE, and revolutionized football

HB Run/Pass

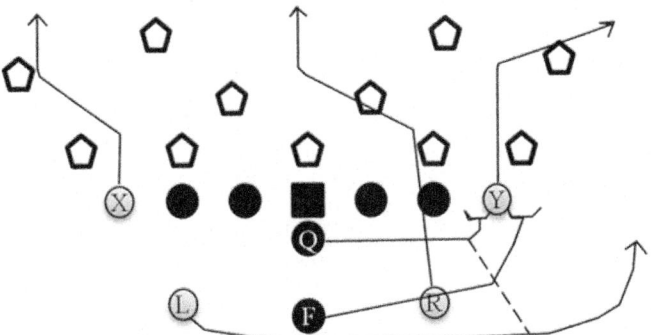

Theme: Run/pass option from option run look; gave HB easy right to left read

Jump Pass

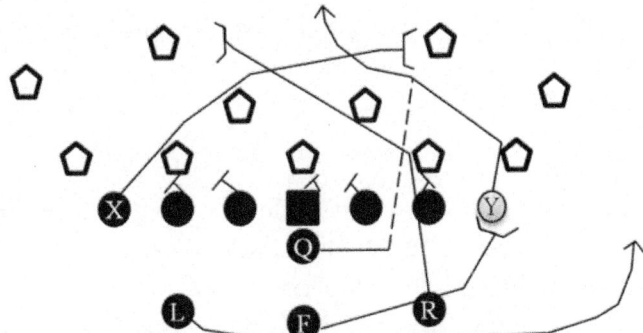

Theme: Jump pass is hard to execute, but kills aggressive run D if executed well

Wing T

Basic alignment:

There are many varieties of the wing T. A "classic" formation has two running backs in the backfield at an even depth (one behind the quarterback and one behind a tackle), one tight end, one wing, and one wide receiver. The wing T can be run with only one back, and has been integrated to shotgun and pistol offenses.

Brief description:

The wing T is a series based run offense that seeks to put individual defenders in conflict. It relies upon misdirection and sleight of hand to keep the defense off-balance and to get superior blocking at the point of attack. While primarily a run-based attack, it features a well developed and often lethal passing scheme to keep the defense honest. Agile "pulling guards" are a well known feature of the wing T and are key components of the offense. The wing T has been a staple since the 1950s, and shows no signs of slowing down.

Good for:

Teams with quick offensive linemen and a quarterback who is athletic and possesses good ball handling skills. The linemen do not need to be big or overpowering, and the quarterback does not need to have a huge arm. Great athletes at the guard position make the offense go.

Bad for:

Teams without a good set of athletic pulling guards will struggle. Some players will be resistant to the offense because it is not what they see on Saturdays and Sundays.

Advantages:

This is a proven "system" offense that has been successful for decades. If you install the system and stick to it, you will see results.

The offense will help you control the ball with both power and deception.

3-4 eligible receivers near the line of scrimmage can threaten the vertical pass defense immediately.

Despite being a running offense, the waggle pass is one of the better plays in all of football.

There are many wing T resources online and in the coaching community.

The wing T can be successful for most youth and high school teams because it does not require prototypical offensive linemen or skill players.

Drawbacks:

Despite the deception of the offense, it can be predictable. If the defense takes away key wing T plays - such as the buck sweep or belly - the coach must know how to make the correct adjustments, and the team must be able to execute them.

The offense is not balanced: if the defense can stop the run game, a wing T team will be hard pressed to win with the pass.

The lack of balance makes a comeback more challenging.

Where it will work:

The wing T can still find great success at the high school level and with youth teams that have enough practice time to perfect it. It can also find success at the small college level. Elements of the wing T have been adopted at all levels of play.

Where it won't work:

The traditional wing T will not be used in the NFL or Division 1 college football because of the speed of defenses and the lack of willingness to commit to the offense.

Defenses that it will beat:

Undisciplined and/or slow defenses will struggle against the wing T.

Defenses that it will struggle against:

A fast, disciplined defense can give the wing T fits. Because wing T offenses often feature smaller linemen, the defense does not need to be huge to win.

Final Word:

The wing T has been successful since the 1950s, and it will continue to be successful. There is a strong community of wing T coaches who swear by the offense, and for good reason. It has a strong identity and a systematic plan for attacking a defense. It does not require spectacular athletes, but does require complete commitment to an unbalanced scheme. It is only recommended for coaches who will commit to mastering that scheme.

Buck Sweep

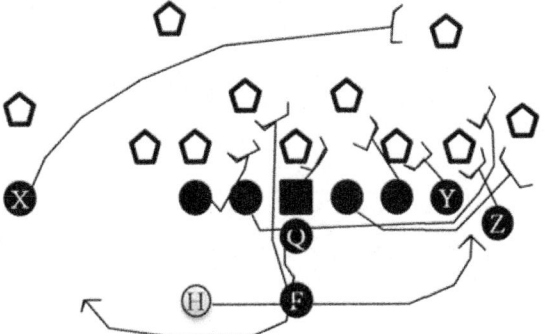

Theme: Down blocks across the line and two pulling guards; a wing t signature

Buck Series Trap

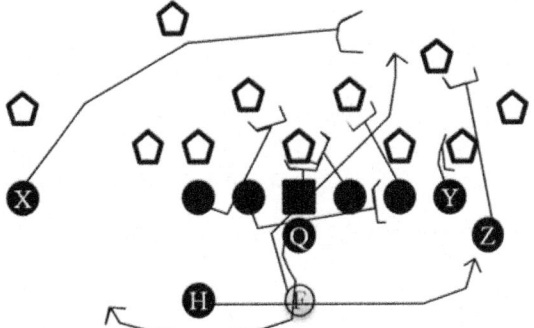

Theme: Defense sees buck sweep keys; QB sleight of hand helps this trap go

Waggle Pass

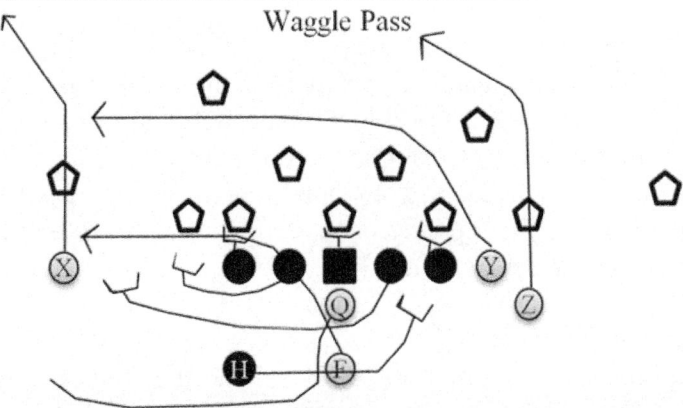

Theme: Deception and QB run/pass threat essential to buck series; a staple play

I formation (traditional/non-option based)

Basic alignment:

Quarterback under center, fullback behind the quarterback, tailback behind the fullback. Most often one tight end and two wide receivers.

Brief description:

The traditional I is a balanced offense that gives flexibility and power in the running game. This is because - with both backs directly behind the quarterback - the offense has the ability to run to any gap with a lead blocker, without giving anything away by alignment. This power at the point of attack in a balanced package makes the I formation a staple at all levels of football. It is perhaps the most well known - and most popular - formation in modern football.

Good for:

The I formation is particularly good for a team with a talented running back. Unlike other two back offenses, the tailback is the clear number one runner in the I. The fullback lead blocks, catches the ball out of the backfield, and gets the occasional carry. The tailback has a personal lead blocker and will get most of the carries, making the I a perfect offense to showcase a terrific back. It can work from year-to-year with changing talent, because the I formation functions with bullish power backs, outside the tackle speedsters, or anything in between.

The quarterback should be an above average thrower. The I formation does not spread the defense, and the quarterback is under center. This makes his reads less clear than out of the shotgun or in the spread. The run game is made possible in part by balance in the pass game. If your quarterback can't make throws in the pocket or off of play action, the defense will be able to beat you with numbers in the box.

This is a great offense for teams with prototypical talent, because this is a prototypical offense. If you have a good quarterback, a talented runner, a good fullback, a real tight end, and two solid wide receivers, and a strong line, the I can showcase them all.

Bad for:

Teams that don't have a traditional quarterback, or traditional skill players, will not get the most out of what the I-formation has to offer.

Teams that are overmatched won't get a huge boost from the I.

Advantages:

A lead blocker in the running game can attack any gap along the front without giving anything away by alignment.

Takes advantage of prototypical talent.

Highlights the talents of tailbacks.

The offensive line can get help from lead blockers and extra pass protectors.

The I formation is run/pass balanced, so a team can grind the clock or make up large deficits through the air in the I.

Many run and pass concepts can be incorporated into the I formation.

The I is flexible enough to highlight athletes at different positions from year to year.

Drawbacks:

If you have less talent than your opponents, the I formation will not help you to even the playing field.

Because of the balance, I formation teams can struggle to establish an identity. Because so many concepts can be incorporated into the offense, there is a temptation to install more than the team can execute.

If you don't have a good thrower, the run game can be controlled with numbers.

Where it will work:

At all levels of play.

Where it won't work:

There is no level of play where the I won't work.

Defenses that it will beat:

The I formation can beat a defense with power, speed, or through the air, so there isn't a particular defense that it can or can't beat.

Defenses that it will struggle against:

The I formation can beat a defense with power, speed, or through the air, so there isn't a particular defense that it can or can't beat.

Final Word:

The I formation is one of the most balanced and successful offenses in modern football. It can be run at all levels, because it can be successful with simplicity and few plays, or with complexity and hundreds of plays. You won't get a great schematic advantage from the I formation, but if you have the players to match up with your opponents, the I is a great choice. You'll be able to win on the ground or through the air, and will showcase talent in traditional roles. If you have a team with a talent disadvantage, however, this is not the offense to help you even the playing field.

USC Sweep

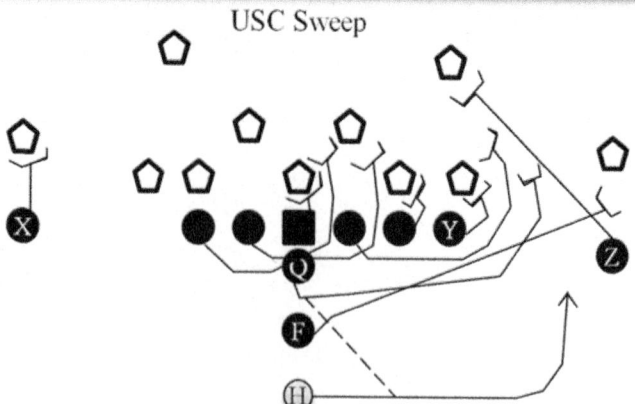

Theme: "Student body right" highlighted great USC tailbacks of the 60s and 70s

Double Tight Iso Weak

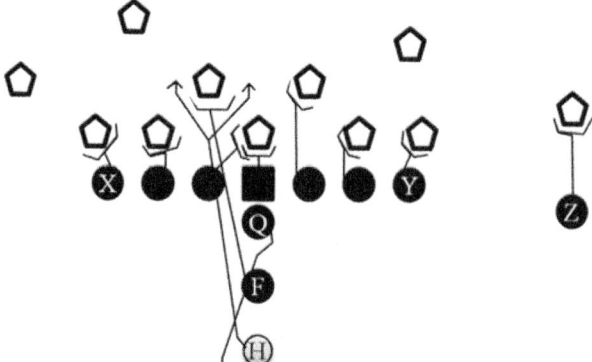

Theme: Double team at point of attack and FB lead power this smashmouth staple

Iso Pass

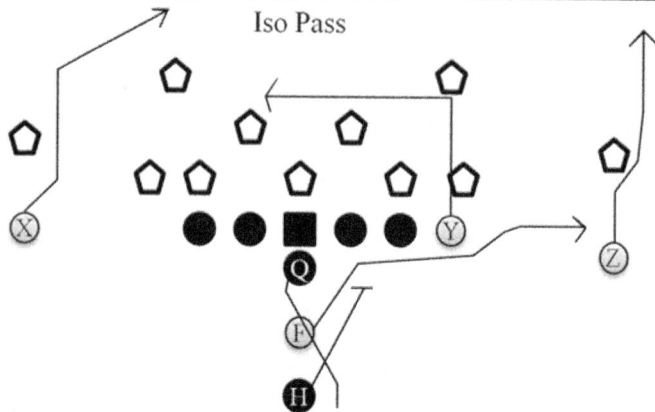

Theme: Play action punishes defenses for selling out to stop the strong I run game

I formation (option based)

Basic alignment:

Two backs lined up directly behind the quarterback, usually one tight end and two wide receivers. Sometimes a wingback replaces one of the receivers.

Brief description:

The option based I formation has enjoyed great success in college and high school football. At its best, it combines the power running of the I with the misdirection and speed of the option. This combination is difficult to defend, because over aggressiveness on the front seven will lead to big plays in the option game, while a passive approach to better defend the option will allow the line to thump the defensive front backwards. Add in the capability of a balanced passing game, and it becomes clear why the offense has been a staple of football for decades. Tom Osborne and the Nebraska Cornhuskers built a dynasty with it, and while it is no longer in vogue with the rise of the spread offense, it remains a potent attack that should be considered a contrarian approach to the spread revolution.

Good for:

A smart running quarterback with a decent arm is a necessity. A good tailback (or two) that can hit the option creases with speed is a major plus. The offensive line should be a grinding, quick, intelligent bunch. The line doesn't need to be big. Bruising fullbacks, blocking tight ends, and prototypical wide receivers will thrive.

Bad for:

A team without at least a little speed at the quarterback and tailback position will struggle. These players don't have to be burners, but must be able to make a decision, plant a foot, and slice through vertical lanes.

The offensive line doesn't need to be big, but it must be athletic enough to cut off front seven pursuit, and strong enough to hold their ground. If you have more power on the line, you can utilize a more power based run game (like Nebraska during the Osborne era).

Advantages:

The offense is option based with the potential for balance, so it can suit changing talent from year to year. The option can help a small, quick team to compete and thrive in the run game, while the power elements are perfect for a group of road graders.

The offense has quick strike capability, but will also dominate the clock. You'll get the benefit of a running offense, but you aren't as crippled when facing a deficit as with other run first offenses.

You get all the benefits of the traditional I running game, with the addition of the option game.

Drawbacks:

Because the attack is varied, execution may suffer.

The option takes a strong commitment. Without knowledgeable coaching and plenty of repetition, turnovers will ensue.

Where it will work:

Colleges, high schools, and youth programs with enough practice time.

Where it won't work:

NFL teams will not expose top QBs to I formation option abuse, and the defenses are fast enough to render it ineffective.

Defenses that it will beat:

Defenses that are undisciplined, slow, or can't defend the point of attack will suffer.

Defenses that it will struggle against:

A speedy front 7 that can stand up against a power running game will give this offense fits.

Final Word:

The option based I formation is a proven offense that has fallen out of favor, coinciding with the rise of the spread. Many teams that formerly ran the option out of the I formation have transitioned to the zone read out of the shotgun. While there are clear benefits to the spread, it cannot replicate the downhill power at the point of attack that the I provides. If you don't have the personnel for the spread, or you wish to embrace a contrarian approach, consider the I formation. You'll have a balanced, old school option attack that will be a change of pace from the spread, providing extra power at the point of attack and a scheme that defenses accustomed to the pace of the spread will struggle with.

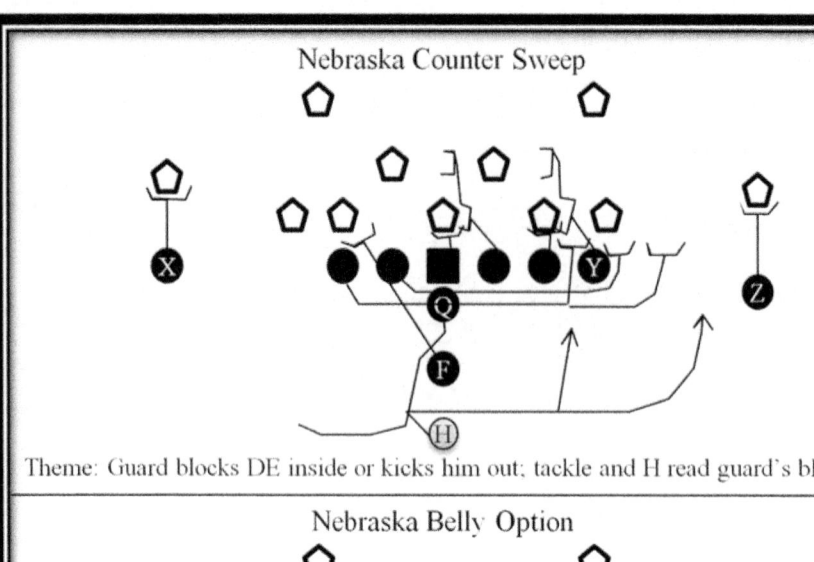

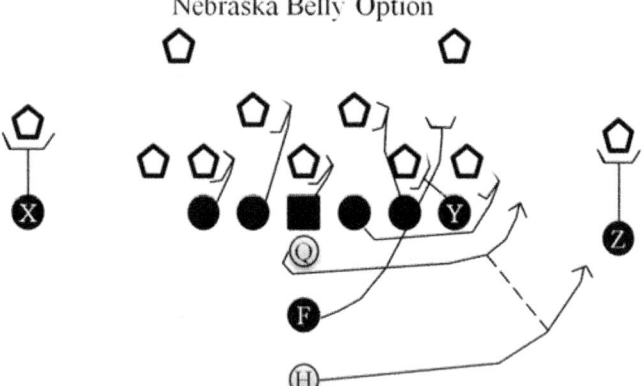

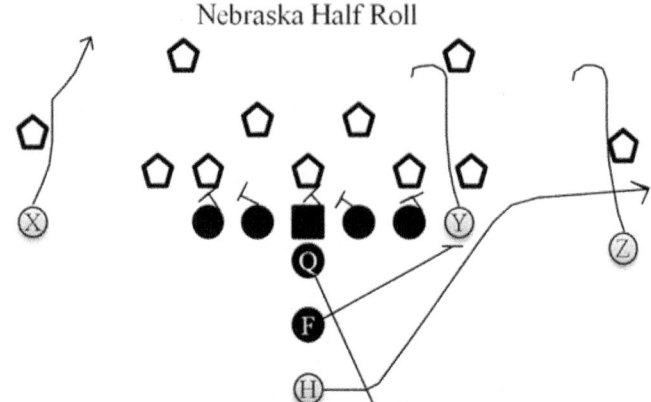

Power I

Basic alignment:

Three running backs: a fullback behind the quarterback, a tailback behind the fullback, and an additional fullback behind one of the tackles. Ranges from two tight ends to two wide receivers.

Brief description:

The power I is a power running offense. It relies on brute force at the point of attack, with two lead blockers. It is a classic youth formation because of its simplicity and running prowess.

Good for:

Teams with power at the line of scrimmage, as well as strong, tough running backs. If your team is strong and knows how to run hard and block with good fundamentals, it can work for you.

Bad for:

Teams that do not have the ability to win battles at the line of scrimmage should look elsewhere. This is not a good offense if you cannot overpower your opposition.

Advantages:

With two fullbacks in front of the tailback, the offense can run inside, off tackle, or outside with two lead blockers. The fullbacks also give the running game the chance for quick hitters.

The offense can use any strategy used by I formation teams, but with an extra blocking back available.

Great for short yardage. Your team will develop a hardnosed identity.

The defense will need to load the box to stop the offense, leaving your receivers with favorable coverage. Play action passing is potent.

The power I is easy to install and is easy for kids to understand.

When the offense is working, you will win the time of possession and will tire the defense with the run game. Staying with the run will pay off late in games.

Drawbacks:

The offense is predictable. If the defense is stronger than you at the point of attack and shuts down the running game, the offense will struggle. It is not known for its misdirection or creativity.

With three running backs, the defense is only faces two immediate vertical passing threats.

Where it will work:

Youth teams, overpowering high school teams, and in short yardage situations in college or the NFL.

Where it won't work:

The offense is too predictable and inflexible to work in the NFL, in college, and at the majority of high schools. However, there are a handful of successful high school programs that use the offense to bludgeon the opposition.

Defenses that it will beat:

Defenses that are weak up front and cannot stop the run will be crushed by this offense.

Defenses that it will struggle against:

Defenses that are physical up front and can stop the run will thrive against a power I opponent.

Final Word:

The Power I is a great youth offense. The plays are simple to understand, and an organized youth team with good fundamentals will have great success with it. The offense only requires 4 or 5 power running plays, a misdirection run or two, and a few passing plays to be successful. On higher levels of play, the power I will only thrive if the players are more physical than their opposition. If your team is more powerful than your opponents, you'll have fun crushing their will with this scheme. It can work as a short yardage formation at any level, and won't require much extra coaching.

Power

Theme: Sledgehammer power at the point of attack off tackle

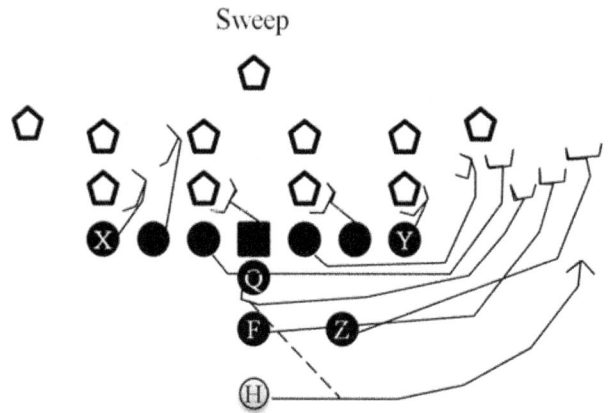

Sweep

Theme: Speed and power to attack the perimeter of the defense

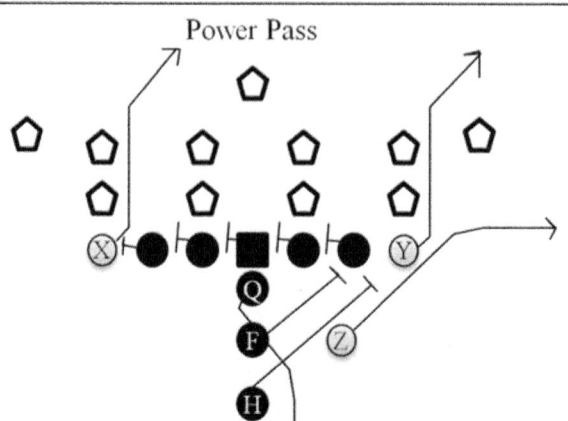

Power Pass

Theme: Play action passing can yield big yards in this run first offense

Split back veer

Basic alignment:

Split backs, one tight end, two wide receivers. Usually wide (3 foot) line splits, backs lined up over the guards at approximately 4 yards depth.

Brief description:

The split back veer is a triple option offense predicated on hitting the line of scrimmage with speed. Defensive linemen are left unblocked and optioned by the quarterback (like the split T), thus allowing offensive linemen to block linebackers and safeties. This downfield blocking is the key, and makes the veer a "big play" running offense. Corollary plays are quick hitting and often utilize misdirection. Because of the run game, defenses often bring eight men into the box. This leaves favorable matchups in the passing game. Although the veer is a run first offense, the two wide receiver, one tight end alignment allows the offense to employ traditional passing concepts.

Good for:

Teams with smart, tough, well conditioned players will thrive. Size is not important. Because the veer leaves players unblocked, the offensive line does not need to win one on one matchups with defensive linemen on every play. Instead, the linemen must be athletic enough to block linebackers and safeties, and get a good initial punch against the defensive line. Acceleration at the snap is key.

You must have a smart quarterback who can make correct option reads more often than not (if he makes the right read 75% of the time, you are in great shape). The quarterback and running backs do not need to be burners, but they must be quick, tough, and willing to run between the tackles.

Bad for:

Teams that want to run a balanced offense.

Teams that have a traditional drop back quarterback who wants to throw the ball.

Advantages:

Big play run offense that does not require exceptional athletes. Proper execution of this offense will allow less talented teams to compete with and defeat more talented teams.

A proven offense that can succeed with almost any type of athlete. If you learn how to execute the offense properly and condition your athletes, you can expect success.

The formation is run/pass balanced (the split back alignment is a traditional passing formation), therefore allowing the incorporation of prototypical passing concepts.

You will have a strong identity.

Not a complex offense.

One of the hardest and most frustrating offenses to prepare for and play against.

Drawbacks:

A coaching staff must fully commit to this offense for it to have any chance of success. The basic option play requires countless repetitions by the quarterback - both in reading his option keys and executing the mesh and pitch aspects of the veer. Don't expect to dabble with other offenses if you install the veer.

Turnovers. Any option offense is more susceptible to turnovers. The "ride and decide" technique, where the quarterback places the ball in the running back's stomach while he reads the pitch key, results in misdirection and big plays, but is prone to fumbles if not practiced with fervor. Suggestion for novice veer coaches: use the "point method." Have the quarterback point the ball at the pitch key. Tell him to give the ball unless the pitch key will make the tackle. If so, the quarterback snaps the ball to his chest before it touches the running back. If the ball touches the running back, the running back takes it. This technique doesn't have as much deception, but cuts down on turnovers.

The offensive line must accelerate with fire on each run play. This makes it harder to pass protect. DO NOT EXPECT TO PASS THE BALL 30 TIMES A GAME IN THIS OFFENSE.

Critics of the veer argue that because the veer is built for the run, it is difficult to come from behind. Veer coaches argue that the big plays in the run game disprove this point.

Where it will work:

High school, college, and youth teams that have enough practice time to master it.

Where it won't work:

Youth programs that have no offseason, and do not practice every day.

The NFL, although veer schemes are now being used out of the shotgun and pistol in the pro game.

Defenses that it will beat:

Undisciplined defenses stand no chance. One missed assignment will lead to huge gains in the running game on any given play. A defense must be able to stop the run to compete against the veer.

Defenses that it will struggle against:

Disciplined defenses with athletic defensive linemen. Athletic defensive linemen kill option plays, because they are fast enough to react to both ends of an option (although a passive approach to defending the option makes a defense more susceptible to traditional drive blocking in the veer).

Final word:

Bill Yeoman introduced the veer with his record breaking Houston Cougars of the 1960s. It became the rage of high school and college football in the 70s and early 80s, evolving into the wishbone, flexbone, and most modern option offenses. Veer concepts have been adapted to the spread option offenses that are the rage in football today, and those concepts are now creeping into the NFL.

Even if the traditional veer isn't used at the major college level anymore, it isn't a thing of the past. It is still one of the most potent offenses in the game, run by record breaking high school powers such as De La Salle (Concord, CA) and John Curtis (River Ridge, Louisiana), and NCAA Division II power Carson-Newman. If you have a hungry group of players without the most natural talent, the veer will win you many games. If you have talent, you'll see big numbers rolling in your direction.

Inside Veer

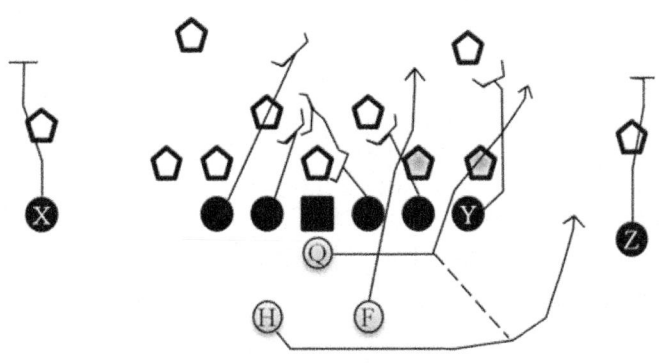

Theme: Wall defense inside; triple option on the first men on or outside the tackle

Outside Veer

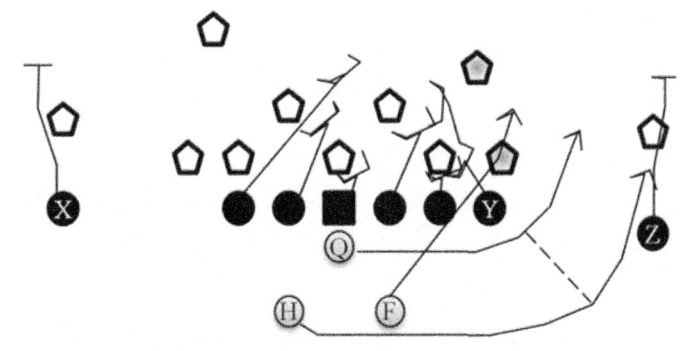

Theme: Option first men on or outside TE; alters defense's option responsibilities

Counter Dive

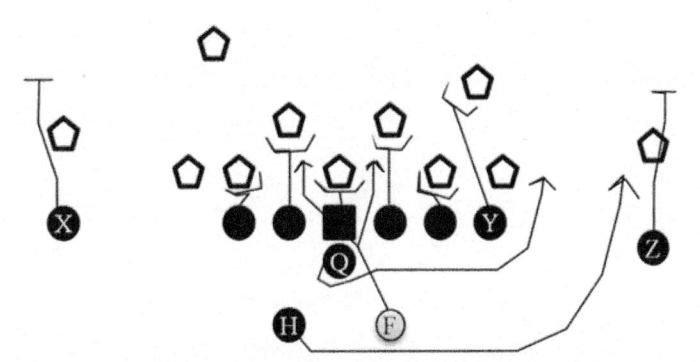

Theme: Hurts fast flowing defenses; can also run counter option with QB/left RB

Wishbone

Basic alignment:

A fullback close behind the quarterback, with two running backs split behind him, over the guards. It can be run with 2 wide receivers, 2 tight ends, or 1 wide receiver and 1 tight end.

Brief description:

The wishbone was developed at the University of Texas in the late 1960s, and soon became the rage in college and high school football. Having evolved from the split back veer, the wishbone is a triple option offense. The addition of the fullback, however, gives the offense one more blocking and running threat. Because the offense features three running backs between the guards and a litany of quick hitting runs, the defense must align to defend the inside run. The offense thrives by then beating the defense to the perimeter in either direction. Like the split back veer, the wishbone is a "big play" running offense, and is responsible for some of the highest scoring teams in college history. The University of Oklahoma still owns the best single season rushing average in history (472 yards per game in 1971) and the most rushing yards in a single game (768 yards v Kansas State in 1988) while running the wishbone.

Good for:

Teams with tough, disciplined and quick offensive linemen. Size is not a necessity. A smart, gritty, and competitive quarterback is a necessity.

Bad for:

Teams who want to throw the ball, or teams with linemen who cannot accelerate.

Advantages:

Like other option offenses, the wishbone is hard to stop when executed properly. The running threats of the veer are present, but with an additional running back to lead block or take handoffs. The run game can do everything from the triple option to misdirection to quick hitters to power plays.

Can chew up the clock and provide big plays.

Allows less talented teams to compete, because defensive linemen can be optioned rather than blocked man-on-man.

By not blocking defensive linemen, offensive linemen are free to block downfield.

Receivers are often left with favorable coverage.

While the wishbone is not balanced in terms of run to pass ratio, there is balance in the ability to spread the ball to four running threats.

Drawbacks:

The offense is not run/pass balanced.

There are only two immediate passing threats near the line of scrimmage.

If not executed properly, turnovers will result.

Where it will work:

Youth programs with significant practice time, high school programs, and small colleges. Despite proven success at the major college level, it is unlikely to resurface in its pure form at that level. This is due to the flexbone taking the place of the wishbone at schools that run a triple option offense.

Where it won't work:

The NFL. The wishbone takes a commitment to an unbalanced offense that an NFL team will not make. It also will not work on youth teams that don't have enough practice time to perfect it.

Defenses that it will beat:

Undisciplined defenses will struggle against the option. A defense that can't stop the run will not compete against the wishbone.

Defenses that it will struggle against:

A disciplined defense with an athletic and stout front seven.

Final Word:

Many youth coaches install the wishbone to run the ball up the middle. Do not fall into this trap. For the wishbone to be successful, it must threaten the interior of the defense while having the ability to beat it to the flank. The triple option does both - on the same play - which is why it is essential to the success of the offense. If you want to run power, stick with the Power I (where you have two lead blockers in front of your tailback). If you have the expertise to install the triple option and will commit completely to it, the wishbone is a proven offense that will roll up the points.

Inside Veer

Theme: Wall defense inside; triple option on the first men on or outside the tackle

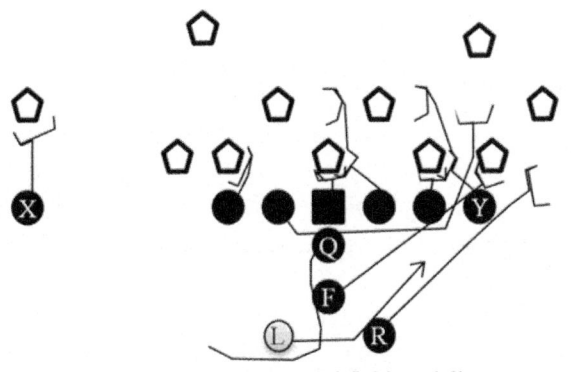

Wishbone Power

Theme: Takes advantage of three man backfield to deliver great power

Fullback Trap

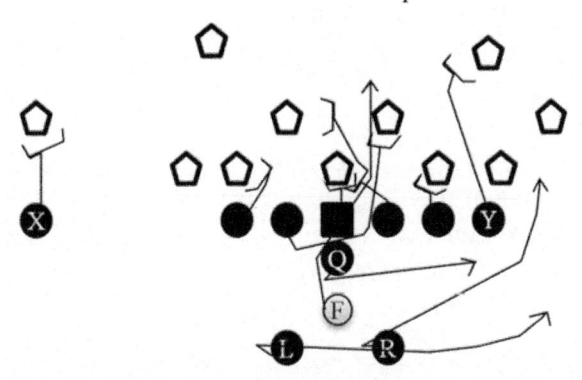

Theme: Quick hitter with sly handoff and angle blocks yields consistent yards

Flexbone

Basic alignment:

A fullback close behind the quarterback, two wing backs, and two wide receivers.

Brief description:

The flexbone is derived from the wishbone (it is a *flex*ible wish*bone*), with wingbacks replacing the deep running backs. This gives extra flexibility with four immediate receiving threats instead of two, and allows flexbone teams to incorporate run and shoot passing principles. The base play of the flexbone is still the triple option (with a quick wingback motion), but flexbone teams have advanced the repertoire, with plays such as the midline option (optioning the first defensive linemen on or outside the guard, instead of the first defensive linemen on or outside the tackle) and the rocket sweep (a quick toss to a fast motioning wingback, instead of a quick toss to a stationary split back). The offense has become a staple at the service academies and throughout high school football. Recently, it has been incorporated into the pistol formation, giving it even more passing flexibility. The flexbone utilizes an "if-then" playcalling methodology ("if" the defense does something, "then" the offense has a play to exploit it), which makes it hard to adjust to and simplifies offensive play calling.

Good for:

Teams with smart, athletic, and tough offensive linemen. Small, quick athletes thrive at the wingback positions, and these athletes are easier to find than true lead running backs. As the offense relies upon intelligence and discipline over athleticism and strength, it is a great offense for outmanned teams.

Bad for:

Teams with prototypical talent may be better off with a prototypical offense. Despite the 4 immediate receiving threats, this is still an unbalanced offense due to the amount of time needed to master the running game and the necessity of a running quarterback. The flexbone passing game is complete and can win games, but a flexbone offense is not in its comfort zone if it must pass first.

Advantages:

A ball control, big play option offense that spreads the defense more than any other triple option offense.

Despite not being balanced in terms of run to pass ratio, there are four immediate receiving threats near the line of scrimmage. A coach can find balance in the flexbone by spreading touches to many athletes.

There is a large flexbone coaching community. If you are an inexperienced coach and your program has some money, you can pay a flexbone expert to come to your field, install the offense, and teach you and your team how to execute it (and no, the author of this book is not affiliated with any such expert). This takes some of the fun out of being a coach, but chances are that you will find success if you follow the plan.

Drawbacks:

Not a balanced offense in terms of run to pass ratio. If a team devotes all the time it should to the running game in this offense, the passing game is left behind.

Turnovers in the option game are a concern if there is not good execution.

Quarterbacks take a beating; traditional quarterbacks may not be happy in the offense.

Where it will work:

Youth teams with enough practice time, high school, all levels of college.

Where it won't work:

The NFL, and youth teams without enough practice time.

Defenses that it will beat:

Undisciplined and/or slow defenses.

Defenses that it will struggle against:

Defenses with an athletic and disciplined front seven.

Final Word:

The flexbone is a proven offense that will not be shut down if executed properly. It may not be the best fit for a team with prototypical talent, but for the vast majority of high school teams, it is an offense that can be run year in and year out with good results. A flexbone team that executes well will rarely be a losing team, regardless of talent. Add good talent to the mix - especially at the high school level - and you will see championship teams. The offense requires a complete commitment - there can be little dabbling in other schemes - but the payoff is consistent. The ability to adapt the offense to the pistol formation is an exciting development that may give even more flexibility to the offense. The bottom line: if you have the practice time and commitment level, few offenses will give a more consistent output regardless of the talent you have.

Inside Veer

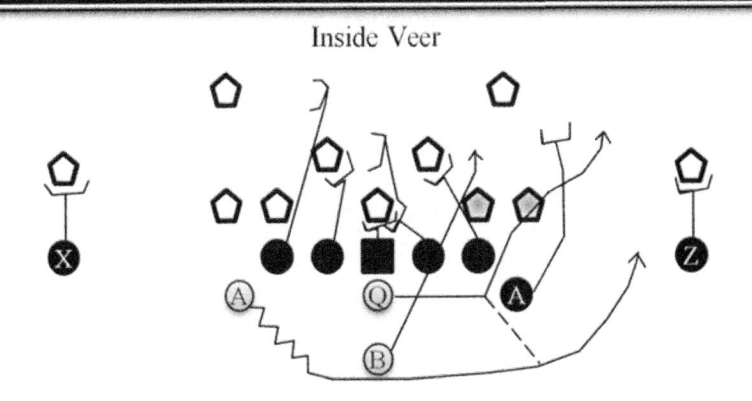

Theme: Wall defense inside; triple option on the first men on or outside the tackle

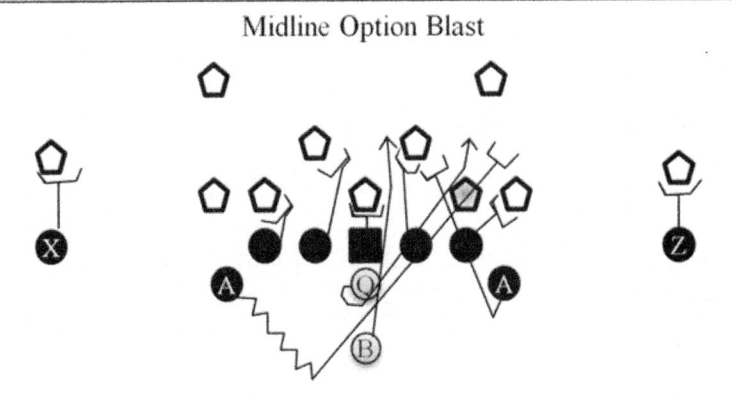

Midline Option Blast

Theme: Option first man on/outside guard; dive hits hard, QB blast has big power

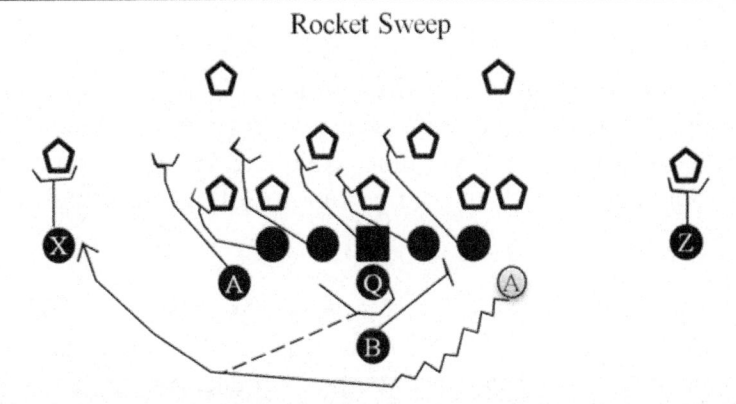

Rocket Sweep

Theme: If the defense overloads the inside, this will kill them to the outside

Double Wing

<u>Basic alignment</u>:

Two tight ends, two wing backs, tight line splits, and a fullback close behind the quarterback.

<u>Brief description</u>:

The double wing is a power running offense that relies on the "toss" play. One wing goes in quick motion, receives a pitch, and follows a litany of lead blockers: two pulling linemen, a fullback, a wingback, a tight end, the quarterback, and half of the offensive line. Only the tight end remains backside. In short, the "toss" bludgeons the point of attack with numbers.

The formation is balanced, so the toss can be run to either side.

The defense is susceptible to interior counters and reverses. The ball is hard to find, increasing sleight of hand.

With 4 passing threats near the line of scrimmage, the pass must be respected.

<u>Good for</u>:

Teams with power at the line of scrimmage. It is a good offense for teams that don't have many players, because it dominates time of possession and does not consume much energy. It can crush the will of an opponent; the "toss" can be run 40 times in a game if it is not stopped.

It can work with big, small, fast, or slow offensive linemen, and does not require a throwing quarterback. It is good for small high schools that can't depend on a consistent type of athlete or a huge roster.

The offense is good for teams with dark jerseys who play at night. If you have such a team, wear your dark jerseys and dim your lights. The other team won't find the ball.

Bad for:

Wide receivers and traditional quarterbacks will not like this offense. Although the pass can be successful, it is mostly a one dimensional offense.

Advantages:

One of the strongest rushing attacks ever devised. It does not require many plays, so it is great for youth teams as well. It is an equalizing offense for small schools or less talented teams. It does not require great athletes to be successful. Execute this offense, and rushing records will fall.

Few turnovers.

Your team will have a strong identity.

If you do have good talent and power up front, it is a very hard offense to contend with.

Your defense will become good at defending the run by practicing against this offense.

Allows a team to play "old school" winning football. Run the ball. Stop the run. Control the clock. Don't turn the ball over. Hit harder than your opponent. A winning recipe that has been around for as long as the game itself.

Drawbacks:

Lack of balance.

Your defense won't play against a traditional passing offense in practice.

There are no wide receiver positions. Wide receivers and throwing quarterbacks won't like this offense.

Where it will work:

Youth teams and at the high school level, particularly among small schools with few players.

Where it won't work:

College, NFL.

Defenses that it will beat:

Defenses that can't hold up at the point of attack will die. Undisciplined defenses will struggle against not only the misdirection, but also the monotonous onslaught of the same play over and over and over and over...

Defenses that it will struggle against:

Defenses that are physical at the point of attack, and which can stop the base "toss" play, will have a chance to beat the double wing.

Final Word:

The double wing is a great offense for youth programs and for high school teams that lack resources. The bludgeoning nature of the offense can lead to big plays and big scoring numbers. If you are a small school, it can give you a chance to be very successful. But it is not only for teams that lack resources. If you are a physical team with good, tough, disciplined athletes, you will have a chance to go far by keeping the ball away from your opponent and putting up points. Many a championship has been won with the double wing. Some players won't like it, but winning silences critics.

Toss

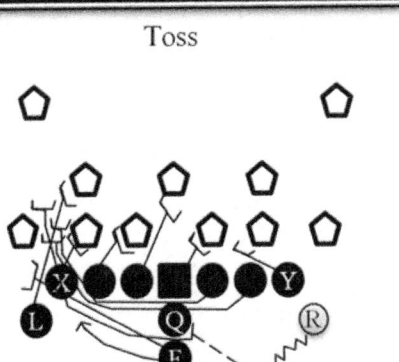

Theme: Down blocks and overwhelming power at the point of attack

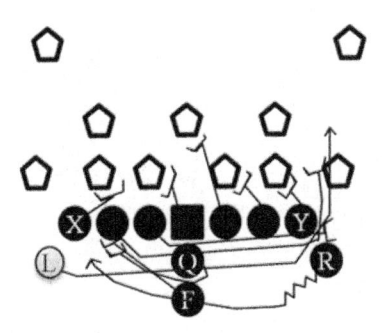

Reverse

Theme: Sneaky powerful counter gets big yards after bludgeoning with the toss

Fullback Wedge

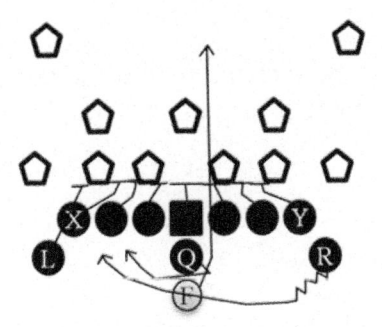

Theme: Quick hitter to fullback a demoralizing show of power with toss deception

Sid Gillman Offense

Basic alignment:

Varied.

Brief description:

"Sid Gillman: Father of the Passing Game," is the apt title of Josh Katzowitz's biography on Gillman. Gillman's influence on the modern game can be seen on every Saturday and Sunday across America. Gillman is largely responsible for introducing timing to the passing game, creating an intricate system of route running in which quarterback drops are linked to each pattern, and the quarterback is instructed to deliver the pass *before* the receiver makes his break. Despite starting his head coaching career in the 1940s, his coaching tree is still alive and well. From Don Coryell and Al Davis to Bill Walsh and the west coast coaching tree, the concepts that Gillman innovated are still at the forefront of the game.

Good for:

A team with an accurate quarterback and enough practice time to perfect an intricate, timing based passing game.

Bad for:

If you don't have an accurate, smart quarterback, and a line to protect the passer, the Gillman attack won't work.

Advantages:

The timing of the passing game creates consistency and big plays when executed properly.

A balanced offense.

Threatens the entire field.

<u>Drawbacks</u>:

The timing in the passing game takes significant time to master.

Many programs can't depend on having an accurate throwing quarterback year in and year out.

You won't have the schematic advantages that Gillman had, because defenses are now accustomed to passing offenses.

Like all balanced offenses, you must work to establish an identity.

<u>Where it will work</u>:

All levels except when players are too young to throw with competence.

<u>Where it won't work</u>:

Youth levels where players are too young to throw with competence.

<u>Defenses that it will beat</u>:

The balance of the Gillman offense means that it can beat any defense.

<u>Defenses that it will struggle against</u>:

A defense should be well rounded to defeat the balanced attack of the Gillman offense.

<u>Final Word</u>:

The influence of Sid Gillman's offense is everywhere in football. In a career that stretched from the 1930s to the 1980s, Gillman went from battling Woody Hayes for recruits in the Midwest in the post WWII years to legitimizing the AFL in the 50s and 60s to telling a youthful Steve Young to play quarterback like the game "is a canvas and you are Michelangelo," introducing and popularizing the basic elements of the modern passing offense along the way. Due to the length of Gillman's career, it is hard to categorize one singular Gillman offense. It is the Gillman concepts that survive. Link the timing of quarterback drops to individual routes. Understand man and zone coverage and know how to defeat each one. Throw the ball before the receiver is open. Utilize running backs in the passing game. Attack the entire field. These concepts can and should be incorporated to every offense that wants to throw the ball with proficiency.

Gillman 181

Theme: Example of quick 3 step timing play that spreads the field

Gillman 444

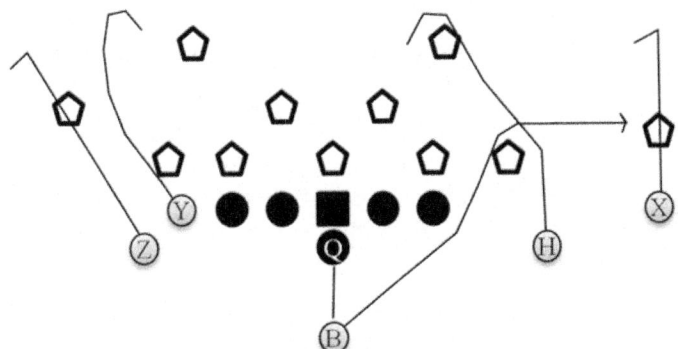

Theme: 5 step medium range timing play kills zones; receivers find the open space

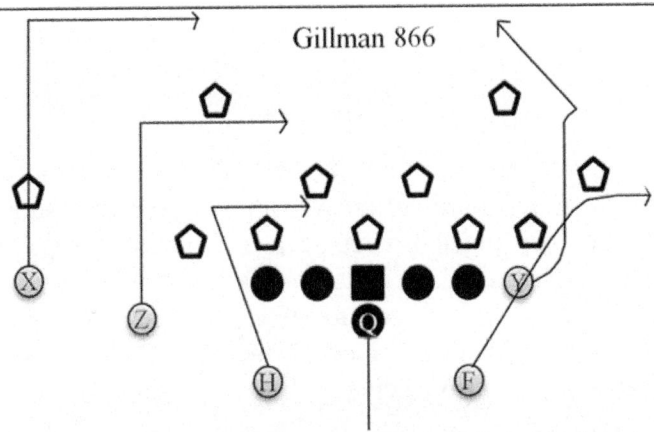

Gillman 866

Theme: This 7 step drop play forces pass defense to be sound from top to bottom

Vertical Offense (Al Davis)

<u>Basic alignment</u>:

Varied.

<u>Brief description</u>:

Known as an outspoken owner, Al Davis's strategic influence on modern football is often forgotten. Like Don Coryell, Davis was a disciple of Sid Gillman. Bill Walsh, in turn, was a disciple of Al Davis. The Al Davis vertical offense shares similarities with their attacks, but is often misunderstood. A vertical stretch does not simply mean that receivers go deep and the quarterback chucks the ball to the fastest one. It means that the defense is being stretched from top to bottom - vertically. A drag by one receiver, a dig by the next, and a post over the top. Or a bench to the flats, a deep out, and a takeoff route. Those vertical stretches force the defense to cover short routes, intermediate routes, and deep routes that flood one third of the field. Speed is at a premium to stretch the defense to the max. The key is not that the deep pattern is hit every time; more often, the vertical stretch opens the field for the intermediate and short routes.

Davis's vertical passing concepts are paired with a power running game.

<u>Good for</u>:

A big armed quarterback and speed at the skill positions are needed for the vertical stretch. This offense requires talent across the board, because the linemen must protect deep quarterback drops, and the skill players must be talented enough to take advantage of everything the offense has to offer. Speed to stretch the field is emphasized more than in other derivatives of Gillman's offense. A stud at running back will also thrive here.

<u>Bad for</u>:

If you don't have a strong armed quarterback and a few players to run under his passes, you won't get the benefits of the vertical stretch in the passing game. Your offensive line must be good enough to protect 5 and 7 step drops with regularity.

Advantages:

Takes advantage of talent and speed on the roster. If you have the quarterback and a few receivers to take the top off the defense, you will get big yards in the intermediate and short passing game, and your power run game will see favorable numbers in the box.

Balanced offense.

Drawbacks:

Relies on offensive talent that most programs won't have year in and year out.

Deep passing game comes with turnover risk.

Where it will work:

It can work at all levels.

Where it won't work:

When the kids are too young to throw far.

Defenses that it will beat:

It can beat any defense. Defenses who are slow in the backfield, or who are not stout against a power running game, will suffer.

Defenses that it will struggle against:

Defenses with speed in the backfield and who can match up physically up front.

Final Word:

The Al Davis vertical offense has taken heavy criticism in recent years. Much of this has to do with several poor personnel decisions on Davis's behalf due to his love for speed and howitzer-armed quarterbacks. But the offense itself is still vital, and one should not ignore Davis's brilliance during much of his career as a coach and owner. The passing concepts have been adopted at all levels, and the theories of timing and vertical stretches are everlasting. If you have good talent and speed on the perimeter, the vertical offense can find great success. In the age of the spread offense, a team that lines up with two backs, smashes the ball between the tackles, and uses time tested drop back route schemes will have an advantage against opposition that is accustomed to the spread pace of play.

Raiders Power Sweep

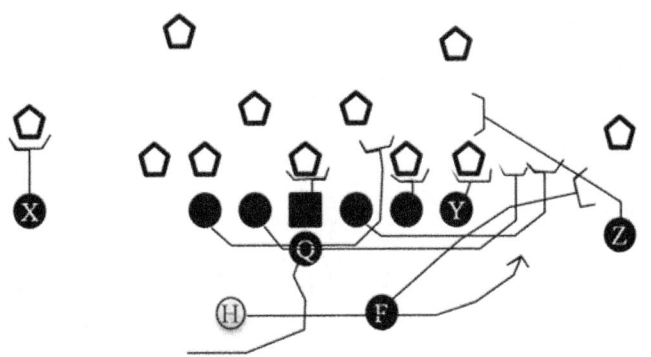

Theme: Hall of Famers Gene Upshaw and Art Shell known for leading this play

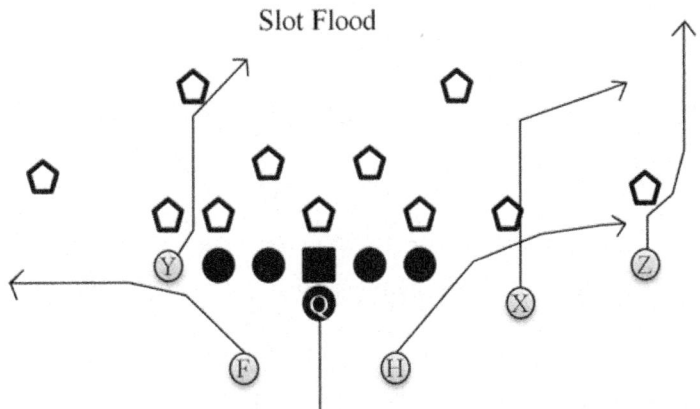

Slot Flood

Theme: Overload to twins side forced D to defend speedy column of receivers

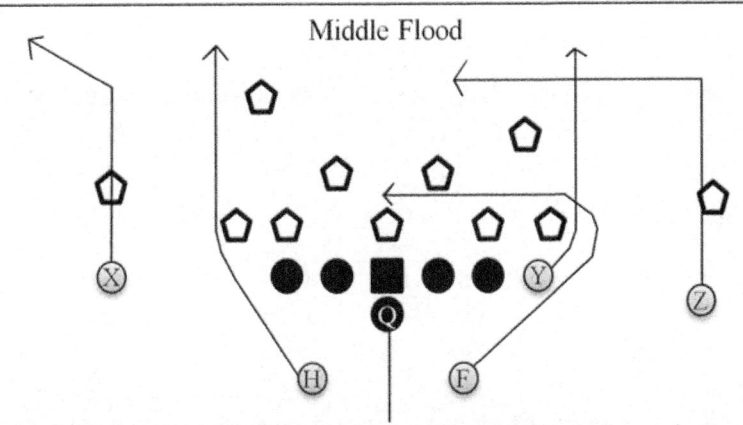

Middle Flood

Theme: Davis loved use of deep in routes by WRs and RBs in the vertical game

Air Coryell

Basic alignment:

Varied.

Brief description:

The original "west coast" offense, few offenses have been as influential as Air Coryell. Like Bill Walsh and Al Davis, Don Coryell was influenced by Sid Gillman's original timing based passing offense. While Walsh learned under Davis (who learned under Gillman), Coryell learned directly from Gillman.

Air Coryell is a power run, vertical passing offense that forces the defense to defend the entire field, whereas Walsh's offense focuses more on horizontal passing, and Davis placed an even greater emphasis on speed and vertical threats. Air Coryell exploded in the NFL during the late 1970s and 1980s, when the Chargers (under Coryell) led the league in passing 6 straight times (1978-1983) and again in 1985, and led the league in combined rushing and passing in 1980-83 and 85. While Walsh's west coast offense enjoys more lasting fame, Coryell's was every bit as prolific.

Good for:

You need talent to run Air Coryell. The quarterback must be able to stand in the pocket and deliver the ball all over the field. He must make good decisions and possess a big arm. He does not need to be an exceptional runner.

You must have good receiving threats. To take advantage of everything the offense has to offer, a combination of burners and possession receivers (or tight ends) is best.

With deep drops in the pocket, a good pass protecting offensive line is necessary.

A power runner will provide balance.

Bad for:

If you don't have a quarterback with a good arm who can make the throws, Air Coryell won't take off. Same for the receivers: if you don't have both speedsters and possession receivers, you won't take advantage of Air Coryell's ability to attack the entire field. Without good pass protecting linemen, your QB can't take the 5 and 7 step drops needed on the vertical concepts.

If you want to throw first, but don't have great talent (or your QB doesn't have a strong enough arm), look to the traditional west coast offense or to the BYU/Air Raid passing offenses. The quick routes and horizontal passing will suit you better.

Advantages:

Forces the defense to cover the entire field: vertically, horizontally, and in the run game.

Takes advantage of all skill players.

Will showcase a traditional pocket passing quarterback.

Run/pass balance.

A systematic, timing based, proven passing offense.

Drawbacks:

If you don't have the right talent, you won't be able to take advantage of Air Coryell.

Where it will work:

At any level where the quarterback has a strong enough arm to work the vertical game. From Joe Gibbs to Mike Martz to Norv Turner, variations of Air Coryell continue to thrive in the NFL. The concepts of Air Coryell will never leave the pro game. Youth teams will need a simplified version, but the numbered passing tree and play calling make memorization more accessible.

Where it won't work:

Youth players without arm strength will have trouble taking advantage of vertical throws, but the timing aspects are great teaching tools for young players. Consider using the numbered passing tree and a few simple passing combinations if you want to use Air Coryell with youngsters.

Defenses that it will beat:

It can beat any defense, particularly those with weak pass defenders.

Defenses that it will struggle against:

A great pass defense will slow the passing game, but Air Coryell is balanced enough to defeat any defense.

Final Word:

Air Coryell is an essential power running, vertical passing offense. Ever since Dan Fouts, Kellen Winslow, Charlie Joiner and John Jefferson took the NFL by storm for Don Coryell's San Diego Chargers, Air Coryell has been synonymous with high flying, high scoring offense. The timing principles should be incorporated into any passing offense, and the concepts are proven. If you have the requisite talent on offense, Air Coryell will take advantage by forcing the opposition to defend every inch of field. If you don't quite have the talent - or if your quarterback doesn't have a strong enough arm - consider passing offenses that focus more on the short, horizontal passing game.

Iso

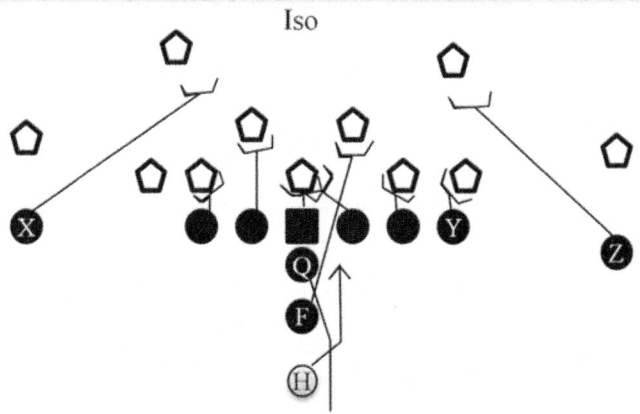

Theme: Classic power football with center/guard double team and FB lead on LB

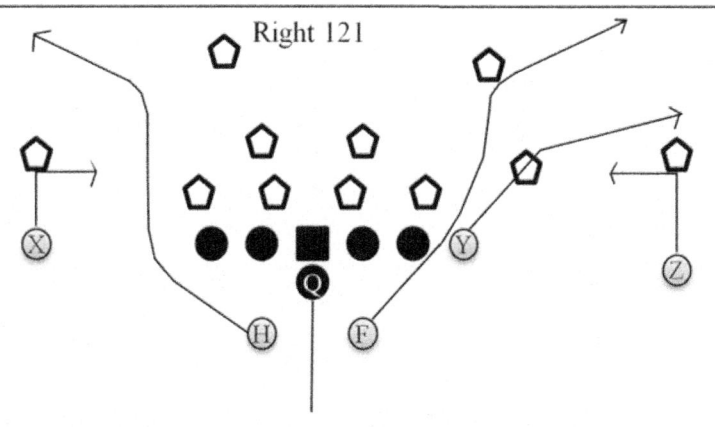

Right 121

Theme: 7 step drop with vertical stretches on both sides of the field

Coryell horizontal stretch

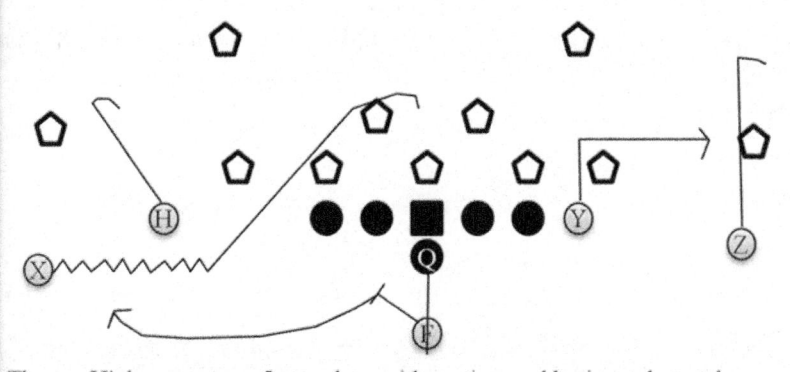

Theme: High percentage 5 step drop with motion and horizontal stretch

West Coast Offense

Basic alignment:

Split backs, one tight end, two receivers, quarterback under center.

Brief description:

The trademark of the west coast offense is a timing based, ball control, horizontal passing game. The brainchild of Bill Walsh, it powered the 1980s San Francisco 49er dynasty and revolutionized the NFL along the way. Walsh's early teams were at a talent disadvantage and could not run the ball against superior competition, so Walsh controlled the ball through the air. The planning of the offense is meticulous - with quarterback steps and footwork linked to the breaks of wide receiver routes - carrying on in the Sid Gillman tradition and creating a machine-like pass first offense. With a focus on the short passing game, big receivers who could break tackles and turn short completions into long gains came into fashion.

Unfairly labeled a "finesse" offense, the running game is also potent. The traditional west coast offense thrived on the power sweep and quick hitting traps and counters. The running backs should have the versatility to run, block, and catch.

Walsh's theories of offense and preparation have spread to all levels of football. While the traditional west coast offense is rarely seen, the concepts and ideologies of the west coast offense are present wherever teams seek to pass the ball.

Good for:

The right fit at quarterback is necessary. He does not need to have size or a big arm. He needs accuracy, athleticism, and good decision making.

Big receivers are a plus, but not a necessity. The key is having receivers who are willing to run disciplined routes, take a few hits, and can gain tough yardage after the catch.

Versatile running backs thrive. Both backs must be able to run, block, and catch.

The offensive line should be agile with the ability to pull and block in space.

Teams with a talent disadvantage can make up the gap with the west coast offense.

Bad for:

If your quarterback is not a good decision maker, don't run the west coast offense. He must have the ability to read coverage, follow a strict progression, and deliver the ball to the correct receiver.

You need a few decent wide receivers with dependable hands.

The quick passing game can alleviate protection issues, but you shouldn't count on the west coast offense if you can't protect the passer.

If you have limited practice time, this is not a good offense for you.

Advantages:

An efficient passing offense that controls the ball through the air. As a ball control pass offense, you'll have more explosive plays than most run based ball control offenses.

Balanced between the run and pass.

The west coast timing principles can and should be applied to any passing offense.

A versatile offense that has an answer to any defense.

Drawbacks:

The west coast offense is complex. For most teams, it is better to choose a few key west coast running/passing concepts and execute them well. The intricacies of the plays and play calls in a professional west coast offense are too much for the vast majority of teams to install and master.

Cover 2, zone blitz, or physical defenses can throw off the timing of the offense.

Where it will work:

The concepts can work at all levels. The professional version of the offense is unlikely to work below the professional level, due to the sheer size of the playbook and the time required to master the timing aspects of so many plays. Pared down versions of the offense can work at lower levels.

Where it won't work:

If you install more principles than your offense can master, it won't work at any level. Although best suited for the NFL, west coast concepts can thrive at every level.

Defenses that it will beat:

It can beat any defense.

Defenses that it will struggle against:

Cover 2/physical defenses can throw off the timing aspects of the passing game. The zone blitz complicates quarterback reads and is a common defense to the west coast offense. But the offense is flexible enough to defeat any defense.

Final Word:

The original Bill Walsh west coast offense is no longer run with frequency. This does not mean that the offense is obsolete. In actuality, the concepts have been absorbed into every NFL (and most other) playbook. If you are going to throw the ball, do your reading on Bill Walsh's practice techniques and methodology.

The pure west coast offense can still thrive, although it is too complex and requires too much practice time for most non-professional teams. When the offense is rolling, the power sweep is as good as any run devised, the complimentary runs are quick and lethal, and no passing game is more efficient. It requires attention to detail, discipline, heavy repetition, and a little bit of talent. If you have those elements, the west coast offense can give you a balanced, winning attack. Most teams should consider a simplified version of the offense, with perhaps 15-20 total run/pass concepts.

Any team can benefit from studying Walsh's problem solving that led to the creation and success of the west coast offense.

Double Slants

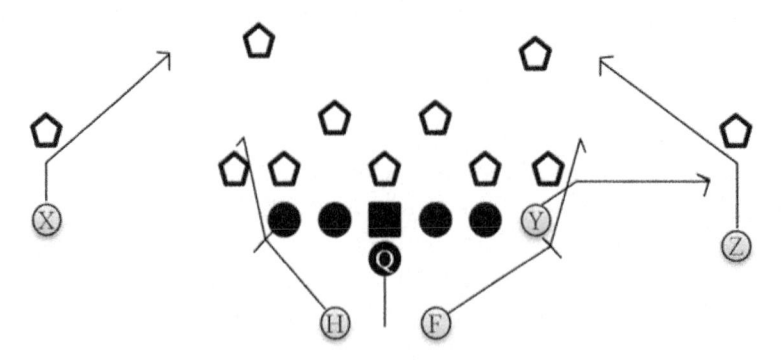

Theme: Indelible west coast image is of WRs turning short slants into long TDs

26 Hook

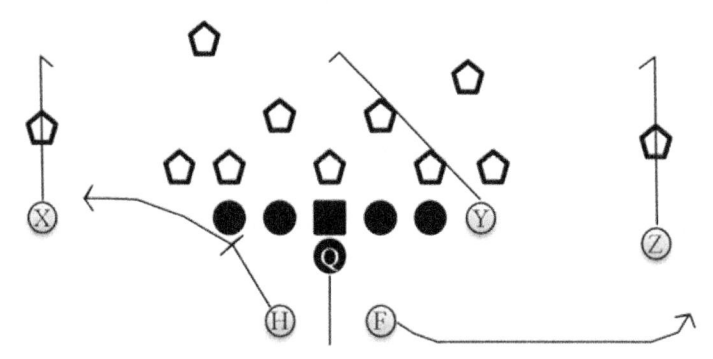

Theme: High % timing play with horizontal stretch and yards after catch potential

49ers Sweep

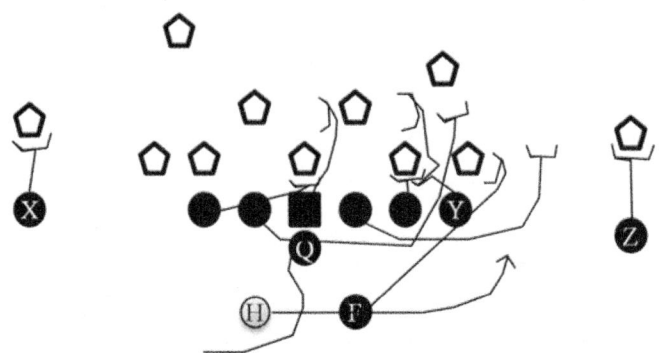

Theme: Classic west coast sweep closely related to Lombardi's famous play

One back

Basic alignment:

One back deep behind the quarterback and four receiving threats (at least two receivers split wide; 0-2 tight ends).

Brief description:

The one back offense is a balanced scheme that spreads the defense to open running lanes and take advantage of four immediate downfield receiving threats. It stresses the defense with the interior and stretch run game, as well as the horizontal and vertical passing game. Thus, it requires the defense to cover the entire field. The plays are not complex, and because the defense is stretched across the field, the quarterback is often left with clear reads in the passing game. While the offense has roots with John Elway's high school days in California, it exploded in the NFL with Joe Gibbs's Redskins of the early 1980s and in college with Dennis Erickson's Miami Hurricanes of the early 1990s (although those offenses were not the same, with Gibbs's version focusing more on a smashmouth run game). Perhaps the greatest example of efficiency in a single back offense is Peyton Manning. His version is among the simplest offense in the NFL, but it works because of the rate at which Manning gets his offense into the correct play at the line of scrimmage to defeat any defense.

Good for:

Teams that have a good quarterback, an offensive line that can block one on one, and fast skill players.

Bad for:

Teams that don't have a competent quarterback or an offensive line that can win individual matchups will struggle.

Advantages:

Balanced offense that can be prolific with the run or pass.

With a good quarterback who can audible at the line of scrimmage, the offense can stay one step ahead of the defense.

Simple plays and a small playbook leave plenty of time to perfect execution.

Spreads the defense to open running lanes.

Attacks the entire field.

Downhill running attack. Zone concepts can defeat a defense with power or finesse.

You can spread the ball to many players with this offense.

Drawbacks:

If you don't have a quarterback who can make correct decisions and accurate throws, don't bother with this offense.

With at least 4 receivers on most patterns, the offensive line must be skilled enough to pass protect without help.

If you can't throw the ball or your receivers can't separate, the defense can shut down the running game with numbers.

Where it will work:

In the NFL, in college, and in high schools with the requisite talent. It can also work in youth programs due to its simplicity, but good throwing quarterbacks at that level are rare.

Where it won't work:

Youth programs who can't yet throw the ball.

Defenses that it will beat:

The offense is balanced and designed to beat any defense. It won't have a huge strategic advantage over any defense, but it won't have a strategic disadvantage in any phase of the game, either.

A defense with backs that can be left alone will thrive, because the running game can be shut down when the defense gains a numbers advantage in the box.

Defenses that it will struggle against:

Defenses that can't cover skill players will struggle.

The one back offense is designed to have any answer to anything the defense might do. This means that overaggressive defenses with schematic weaknesses can be exploited, if the offensive line is good enough to protect and the quarterback can make the right decision.

Final Word:

The one back offense is one of the simplest and most efficient offenses in the game, IF the offense has the right personnel. With a quarterback like Peyton Manning - who can get his offense into the right play and makes terrific decisions - it is almost impossible to stop. Ryan Leaf - who many felt should have been chosen ahead of Manning in the 1998 NFL draft - also thrived in the offense at Washington State. But Peyton Mannings (and Ryan Leafs) do not grow on trees. If you are fortunate enough to have a quarterback and offensive line to run this system, it is one of the best offenses to maximize their talent. You will have the ability to control the ball with the run and short passing game, or compete in high scoring shootouts filled with vertical passing. If you don't have the quarterback or offensive line, look elsewhere.

Inside Zone

Theme: Zone blocking creates creases for RB to run in several directions

Counter Trey

Theme: Similar to power, but RB jab step influences LBs while T leads the way

Inside Options

Theme: Option routes exemplify the space that one back offenses give to receivers

LaVell Edwards BYU Passing Offense

Basic alignment:

Split backs, at least two wide receivers.

Brief description:

LaVell Edwards created his offense in order to compete against physically superior competition. BYU was a losing football program when he was hired, and figuring that he'd be fired in a few years anyways, Edwards took a chance by turning BYU into one of college's first pass first offenses. Edwards favored repetition and execution over complexity. He turned BYU into an offensive powerhouse, produced numerous record breaking quarterbacks, won a national championship, and became one of the winningest coaches of all time. The Air Raid offense grew out of the BYU influence.

The BYU passing offense shares many similarities with the west coast offense. The quarterback drops and wide receiver routes are run in a timed sequence so that the quarterback can throw in rhythm to a set progression. The offense seeks to maintain control of the ball through a high percentage passing game. Both offenses were designed to help a less talented team thrive.

BYU is more pass happy than the west coast offense, throwing the ball 40+ times with regularity. The playbook is simpler, focusing more on repetition than intricacy. The BYU offense tries, at all times, to "KISS" (keep it simple stupid). While the west coast offense is known for the horizontal stretch, the BYU passing scheme is known for attacking the entire field - horizontal, vertical, and Edwards's "oblique" stretches (triangles). The goal is to give the quarterback easy reads and let him make easy throws to take advantage of what the defense gives him.

Good for:

Teams with a smart quarterback, disciplined receivers, and capable pass blockers can run the BYU offense to compete with more talented teams.

No one on the offense needs to be an exceptional athlete; discipline and skill are more important.

The quarterback does not need to have a huge arm.

Bad for:

Teams without an accurate, smart quarterback should look elsewhere. If you don't have the ability to protect the passer, it won't work. If you want to pound the ball with the run, this isn't for you.

Advantages:

Controls the ball in the air, leading to more scoring than most ball control offenses.

Equalizes talent deficits.

Relies on execution more than individual talent.

Simpler than many passing offenses.

With two backs, the run game must be respected, and you have the flexibility to keep extra blockers in pass protection. You can achieve balance.

Drawbacks:

If you don't have the quarterback to throw or the line to protect, you'll turn the ball over and suffer many negative plays.

The run game is not smashmouth. You'll devote most of your time to the pass game, which can weaken your run game and your run defense.

Where it will work:

All levels. The pure form won't be seen in the NFL (although the concepts will endure), while many youth teams won't be proficient enough with the pass to run it.

Where it won't work:

The pure form won't be run in the NFL, and many young players can't pass well enough to run it.

Defenses that it will beat:

Defenses with weak pass defense will struggle.

Defenses that it will struggle against:

Defenses that can cover receivers and pressure the quarterback without blitzing will cause trouble.

Final Word:

The BYU passing offense is a proven winner that has had a great effect on the modern game. Look to any Air Raid offense, and you'll see the BYU influence. Consider also that LaVell Edwards had only one losing season in 29 seasons at the helm of BYU. The offense is built for winning football; high percentage throws, control of the ball, and points on the board. It is simpler than many passing offenses, making it more accessible for younger players and leading to better execution. With two backs in the backfield, the defense must respect the run. If you want an easy passing offense that gives you more flexibility in protecting the passer and developing a ground game and a simpler playbook than the west coast offense, look to BYU. The offense can still succeed in its true form.

H Option

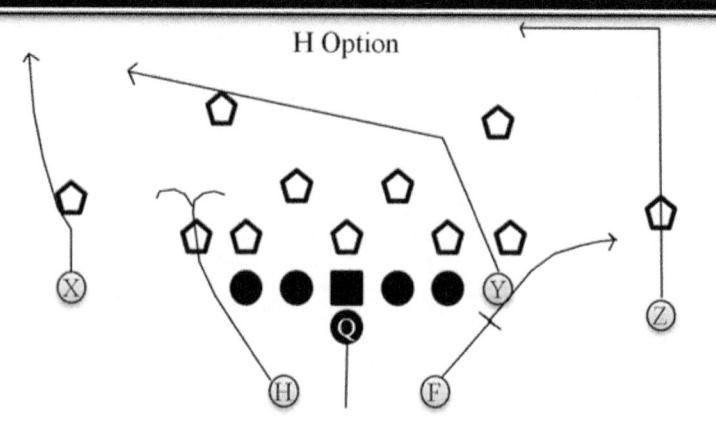

Theme: Example of classic BYU option route also includes famed Y cross pattern

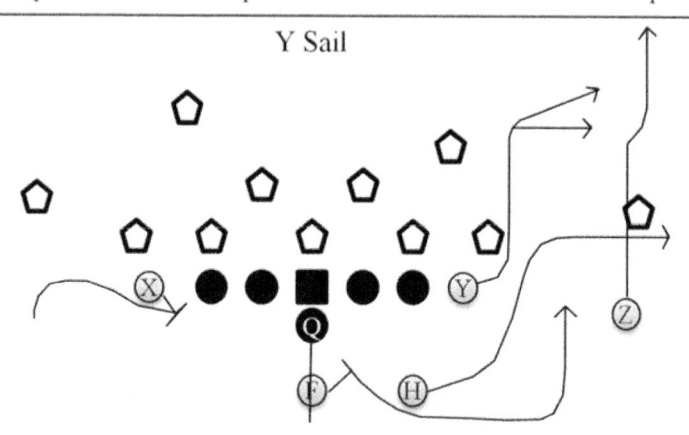

Y Sail

Theme: Variations of this classic flood with Y option remains a staple at all levels

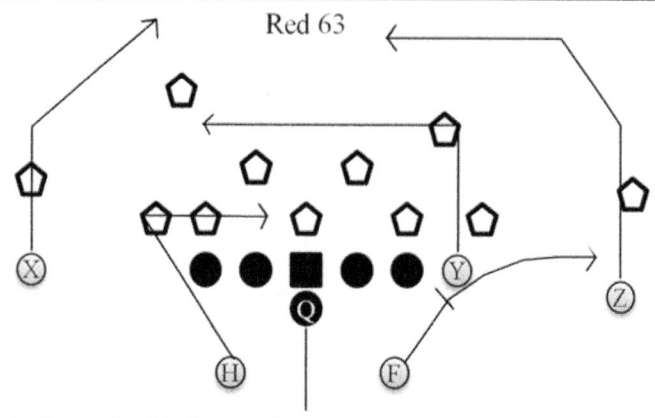

Red 63

Theme: Vertical stretch with 4 routes flooding the middle of the field

Air Raid

Basic alignment:

Traditional: split backs, at least two wide receivers, quarterback under center. Contemporary: varied, often spread, quarterback in shotgun.

Brief description:

The Air Raid grew out of Hal Mumme and Mike Leach's trips to BYU to learn and adopt LaVell Edwards's offense. As Mumme and Leach moved through the college ranks - from the NAIA to the SEC - they tweaked and streamlined the offense. By the time they reached Kentucky (burning through defenses at each stop along the way) they were running an extreme version of what they had learned from BYU. BYU passed the ball often. The Air Raid passed the ball more. BYU was simple. The Air Raid was simpler. If BYU favored repetition and execution, the Air Raid took it to another level. The same drills and concepts are run over and over and over again. Instead of running passing lines with one quarterback and one ball in the air, they run it with five quarterbacks and five balls in the air, thrown in strict adherence to the passing progression. Each quarterback learns the progression to perfection. Every receiver learns one position. The ball is constantly in the air. Receivers catch the ball all practice long. Stretching lines are replaced by passing lines. Execution is perfected. The Air Raid is as much an ideal as it is an offense: choose something to be good at, commit to it completely, and rep it to death. This principle can and should be applied to any offense.

Leach also cites the wishbone as an influence. Both offenses - while not having traditional run/pass balance - find balance in spreading the ball to many athletes and forcing the defense to defend the width of the field.

Over the years, the Air Raid has expanded in various ways. The quarterback is almost always in shotgun now. Some Air Raid teams use 4 wide receivers; others use two wide receivers and a full house "diamond" backfield. Some run the Air Raid at a hurry up no huddle pace. Some have simplified the Air Raid even more, eliminating all unnecessary run/pass plays from the playbook. All of these forms have been prolific. The common thread is the Air Raid passing concepts and the approach to the quarterback progression and practice: simplify reads, attack one defender and throw away from where he goes, and maximize reps in practice.

Other features of the traditional Air Raid are wide line splits (to spread pass rushers away from the quarterback and open passing lanes) and the willingness to run a successful play over and over again. The Air Raid is to the passing game what the double wing toss is to the running game.

Good for:

You need a quarterback who can throw the ball accurately, but he doesn't need a big arm. The offensive line must be able to protect. Your wide receivers need good hands and discipline. Speedy wide receivers are a plus. The slot position is perfect for a small, quick receiver (a la Wes Welker).

The offense doesn't require top end talent, making it an equalizing offense.

Versatile running backs are a plus. While the offense is pass heavy, running backs can thrive in the Air Raid as runners and receivers out of the backfield. If the defense gives the run to the offense, the Air Raid can take advantage.

Bad for:

Teams that want to feature the running game should look elsewhere.

If your quarterback doesn't have good accuracy and decision making, it won't work. Keep in mind that committing to the Air

Raid - and the practice plan - will help cure these problems because of the simplicity of reads and the repetition of the progression.

Advantages:

Practice structure. The Air Raid maximizes repetition and practice time. Even if you don't run the Air Raid, study these drills and consider adopting them for your team.

Prolific passing offense.

Controls the ball through the air, providing bigger plays than many ball control offenses.

Spreads the ball to many skill players, keeping them happy.

While the offense isn't balanced, the running game can threaten. The classic version has two running backs - more than the spread - and running backs can show off their versatility.

You can come back from large deficits with this offense.

The repetitions and execution make it an equalizing offense.

The simple concepts and thin playbook make it an easy passing offense to learn.

Takes what the defense gives, attacks those weaknesses, and does not relent.

Drawbacks:

Not a run/pass balanced offense. If you don't commit to throwing the ball to the extreme, you aren't running the Air Raid.

The other team is never out of a game. If you stop completing passes, you'll lose the time of possession, and the other team can control the clock.

Your defense won't practice against a smashmouth running game.

Because you will stop the clock often with incompletions and scores, the game is extended, and your defensive statistics will suffer.

Where it will work:

All levels (although the pure form is too simple and unbalanced for the NFL). The simplicity and repetitions may make it a great passing offense for youth teams.

Where it won't work:

It is too simple and unbalanced for NFL teams to adopt. It won't work when kids are too young to throw the ball.

Defenses that it will beat:

If a defense can't defend the pass, say goodnight.

Defenses that it will struggle against:

Fast defenses with good pass defenders and the ability to pressure the passer without blitzing.

Final Word:

One of the most prolific offenses ever devised, the Air Raid continues to break records as it changes forms. From the traditional Mumme/Leach version to the simplified no huddle hurry up version that Tony Franklin has spread to the high schools of America to the packaged concepts (for example, a quick route as a first read, and a draw if that route isn't open) and full house backfields of Dana Holgorsen at West Virginia, the Air Raid continues to evolve and put up points along the way. Whether or not you choose the extremes of the Air Raid is up to you. Regardless, we can all learn a lesson from the Air Raid: choose something, commit to it completely, simplify the concepts, and rep those concepts over and over and over and over again.

4 Verticals

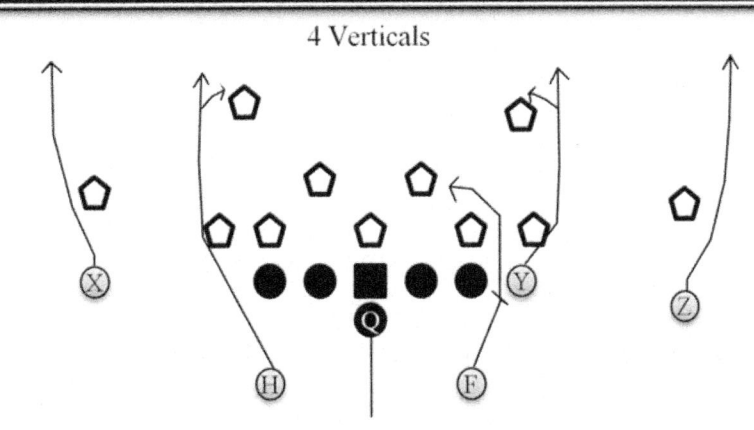

Theme: Forces D to cover 4 deep threats; now more often run with 4 WRs/shotgun

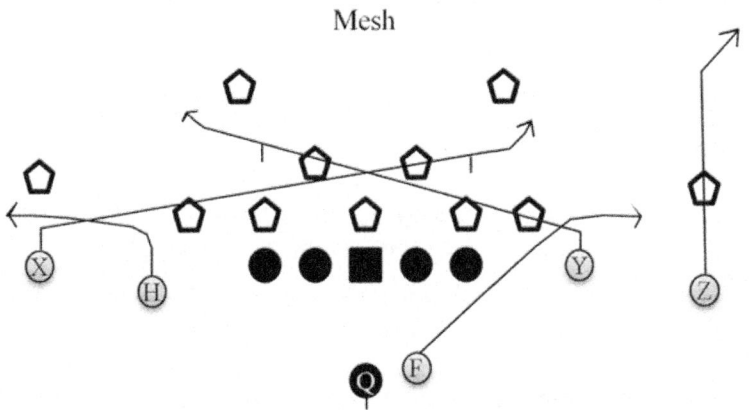

Mesh

Theme: X/Y run away from man with natural pick; v zone find hole after mesh

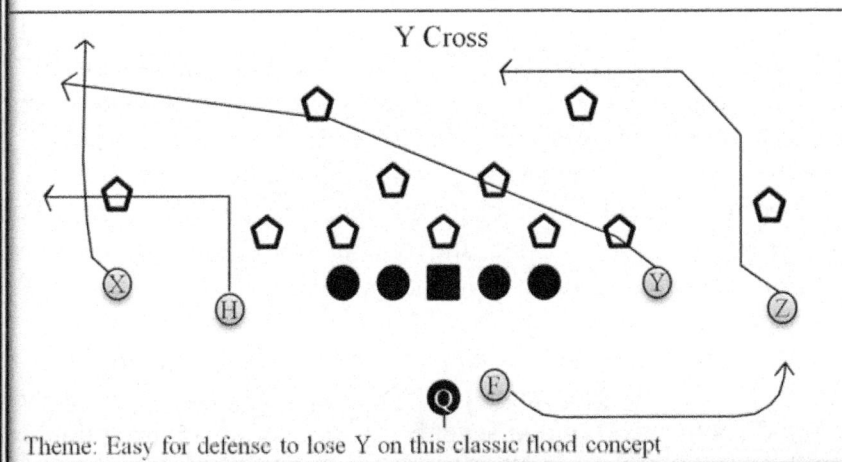

Y Cross

Theme: Easy for defense to lose Y on this classic flood concept

Run and Shoot

Basic alignment:

One back, four wide receivers.

Brief description:

The defining feature of the run and shoot are the "option" routes run by the wide receivers on the fly. After the ball is snapped, the receivers have several options on each play, running a pattern based upon the coverage they encounter. When the QB and wide receivers are on the same page with these adjustments, the passing game is nearly unstoppable. The run and shoot reached its heyday in the 80s and early 90s, when it made its way to the USFL and NFL, and the Houston Cougars rewrote the college record books with it.

Boiled down to its simplest form, the offense is based on schoolyard play: the quarterback runs around, the receivers run to open space, the quarterback hits the open receiver, and everyone has fun. The run and shoot adds structure to that basic formula.

The traditional form of the offense utilizes half or full rolls by the quarterback from under center. This forces the free safety to declare his coverage, and allows the quarterback to attack one half of the field with a run/pass option. The traditional form also incorporated motion from 2x2 to 3x1 sets, to expose coverage and change strengths. Over the years the offense became known as a pass first aerial assault out of the shotgun, with fewer rolls and motions. The number of formations - one back, two receivers on each side (2x2) or three receivers on one side and one on the other (3x1) remains miniscule in comparison to most modern offense.

While the run and shoot is known for its record breaking passing game, it wasn't always intended to be so pass heavy. The original run and shoot incorporated several run series, including option and power running schemes. While this is not the run and shoot offense that most will recognize, one can achieve balance with it. Start your reading with "Run-And-Shoot Football: The Now Attack," by the creator of the run and shoot, Glenn "Tiger" Ellison. To see how the offense has evolved, watch June Jones's SMU Mustangs or clips of his prolific Hawaii Warriors teams.

Good for:

Teams with a good quarterback and smart receivers who have enough time to work together so that the "on the fly" adjustments are perfected.

This is an offense that allows you to compete with less talent.

Because of the half or full rolls in the traditional form of the offense, a team can compensate for a weak offensive line by getting the quarterback outside the pocket.

Bad for:

Teams that don't have a quarterback who can make accurate throws and good decisions on the fly should look elsewhere. If there isn't enough time for the quarterback and receivers to work together on the option routes, or if the receivers can't make the reads, the offense won't work.

Because the ball is in the air with option routes, and the quarterback is often out of the pocket and scrambling, this is a high risk/high reward offense. An inferior team can win more games with it than it should, but a powerhouse might drop a game or two with it if they aren't clicking on a particular day. Teams with prototypical talent might look towards a prototypical offense.

Advantages:

High scoring offense that is fun for players and spreads the ball around. Can compensate for a weak offensive line with quarterback rolls. The option routes are difficult to stop when the correct reads are made.

There are not many formations or plays, so memorization won't be an issue.

If you look into the history of the offense - starting with Ellison - you will see that the offense does incorporate several run series. If you want more balance in the offense, consider the traditional form, with the quarterback under center and a single back. Look to the historical run and shoot run series, or consider incorporating single back running concepts.

Great passing offense.

The spread field opens running lanes.

Attacks the entire field.

The offense is more about how you execute than the skill of your opponent. If you execute, the defense can't stop you.

Drawbacks:

The option routes take significant time and knowledgeable coaching to perfect, so if you want to run this offense, educate yourself and commit completely. Be prepared for it to take time (seasons, in some cases) for your players to thrive in the run and shoot. You may have to lose big before you win big.

If you run the pass happy version of the run and shoot, your running game and time of possession are likely to suffer.

You may have trouble using power on short yardage or goal line situations. Your defense won't practice against a power attack, potentially weakening your run defense.

If you don't have a decent quarterback to run this offense, it won't work.

Where it will work:

NFL, college, and high school, although the pure form is unlikely to show up in the NFL again (though almost every NFL team incorporates run and shoot concepts). Some argue that the Tom Brady Patriots and the Peyton Manning Colts/Broncos run variations of the run and shoot, although not in the pure form.

Where it won't work:

The option routes are probably too difficult for youth players to master. While the option concepts of the run and shoot have survived and thrived in the NFL, the pure form of the offense isn't likely to resurface at that level.

Defenses that it will beat:

Defenses without speed and skill in the secondary.

Defenses that it will struggle against:

Defenses that can rush the passer without blitzing, with enough speed and skill in the secondary to defend the pass, will give the run and shoot trouble.

Final Word:

The run and shoot is one of the great passing "systems" in the game. Ellison created his attack to emulate backyard football and help his undermanned Ohio high school team thrive during the smashmouth days of the 50s and 60s. The run and shoot remains a high powered equalizing offense to this day. With a track record of success, it is nearly impossible to stop when the option routes are executed properly, because they adjust to defeat any defense. Those routes are difficult to master, however, and the offense takes commitment and knowledge over the course of several seasons. Master this offense, and your teams will put up huge numbers, spread the ball around, and will defeat teams that you probably shouldn't. Commit to the offense halfway, and you'll see your turnovers spike, putting more pressure on your defense. If you want to run this offense, go all in, be patient as it develops, and make sure you have the expertise to make it work.

Go

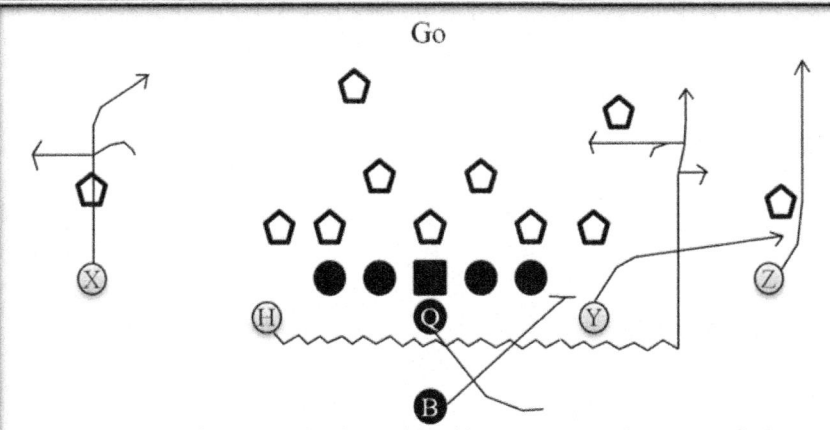

Theme: QB reads flat D; motion helps identify coverage; option routes find space

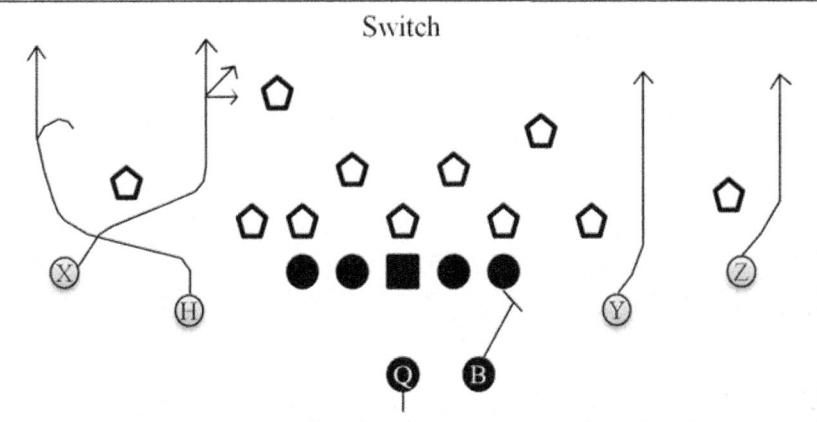

Switch

Theme: Example of vintage R&S option route concept as adapted to shotgun

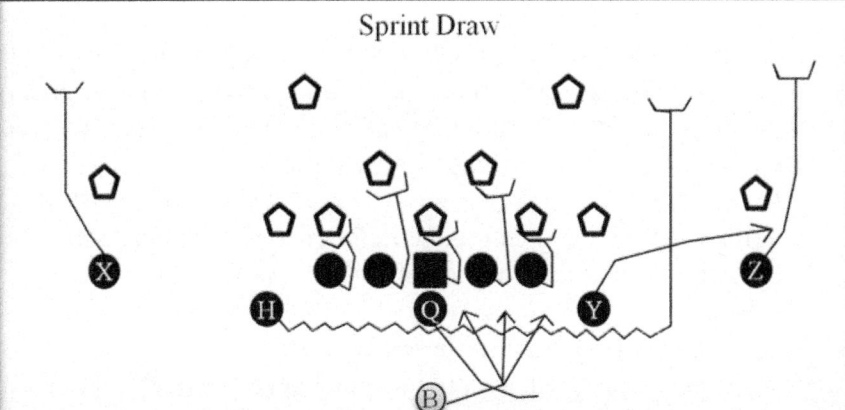

Sprint Draw

Theme: Classic R&S was almost all sprint passes; sprint draw cut against the grain

Spread offense

Basic alignment:

The spread offense spreads the field with receivers, often with one back and a quarterback in the shotgun.

Brief description:

The spread puts pressure on the defense by forcing it to cover the entire width of the field. This spreads the defense thin and allows the offense to get the ball to athletes in space. There are many varieties of the offense, but an overarching theme is stretching the defense horizontally in order to puncture holes vertically. Common plays include the spread option, zone runs, wide receiver screens, and a variety of basic passing concepts. These plays often target a particular defender in space (for example, an outside linebacker or force defender), putting him in conflict and giving the quarterback easy reads based off of his reaction. There are many identities a team can adopt out of the spread, from spreading to run, to spreading to pass with a pocket quarterback, to spreading to run the option.

Good for:

A competent quarterback is a necessity in the spread offense. He can be a better runner than passer, but he must be skilled enough as a thrower to make the defense respect the spread receivers, even if only in the screen game. If the defense knows the offense can't pass, they can defeat the spread run game with numbers in the box.

Fast skilled players who can make defenders miss in space make the offense thrive. The backs and receivers do not need to be big.

Although speed is a bonus, the offense can also be prolific with smart, disciplined, quick receivers and backs. These athletes are plentiful in most programs.

The line must be good enough to win individual battles; the spread alignment ensures that there will not be much extra pass blocking help from backs and tight ends. A decent quick passing game will help a weak offensive line. The quarterback should be able to complete quick passes in the face of unblocked defenders if the defense brings more pass rushers than the offense has blockers.

Bad for:

Teams that don't have a competent quarterback should not run the spread.

Teams that don't have an offensive line that can win individual battles should not run the spread.

Advantages:

If an offense has the right players to run the spread, the spread will take scoring to the next level. It stresses the defense from sideline to sideline, and can be effective as a run first, pass first, or run/pass balanced offense. For this reason it can be adapted year-to-year for changing talent.

The spread offense is named for the spread formation, but it also spreads the ball around to many different players; it will keep skill players happy.

The schemes are not complex. Repetition and execution are essential.

With the scoring of the spread offense, you can come back from sizeable deficits.

The running game is good and receiver routes are high percentage, so you can control the clock with the spread.

If you have skill players who are difficult to tackle in space, the spread will take advantage of their talent.

Drawbacks:

If you don't have a decent quarterback or offensive line, you will have trouble in this offense. The spread puts more players in space in individual matchups; if your line can't win these, nothing will work. If your quarterback can't make proper reads or accurate throws, you will turn the ball over. The quarterback must be good enough to either throw under pressure or escape that pressure.

While spread teams can run the ball, they do not feature the traditional two back, one tight end, smashmouth offense. Your defense won't see much smashmouth football in practice. This may hurt your defense when they play against a traditional power running team.

If your pass game isn't threatening enough, the opposition can beat your run game with numbers in the box.

You may have problems in short yardage situations or in games where you wish to drain the clock, because you won't be accustomed to traditional goal line/running formations. Spread teams are susceptible to comebacks for this reason.

You may lose the time of possession and put pressure on your defense, especially if you are not efficient in a pass first version of the offense.

Where it will work:

The NFL, colleges, high school, and youth teams that are able to complete short passes.

Where it won't work:

The scheme is simple, so players can understand it regardless of age. Skill level is the important factor.

Defenses that it will beat:

Defenses that can't win one on one matchups, be it on the line, covering receivers, or tackling in space, will struggle. Speed is more important than strength against the spread.

Defenses that it will struggle against:

Defenses with speed and players who can tackle in space are best suited to play the spread. Good defensive backs are a must. Versatile linebackers are also important. Defenses that can defend the run with fewer players in the box will give themselves a better chance against the perimeter plays.

Aggressive, blitz on every play, man to man defenses are boom or bust against the spread. Sometimes, they'll give you fits with their pressure. If you can handle the pressure, however, you will exploit systematic weaknesses and get big plays with ease.

Final Word:

The spread offense is the offense of the moment. For good reason. Most spread offenses are not complex; they are based on repetition, execution, and the ability of your players to win in space. With the right personnel, you will put up huge numbers, and you will never be out of a game. Be warned, however, of the spread offense trap. If you don't have the right personnel, you will not be able to compete. No longer is the spread offense a novelty that will help an undermanned team defeat a surprised opponent. It is easy to be tempted by the spread offense when watching high scoring teams on Friday nights or Saturdays or Sundays or when analyzing the offense from an x's and o's standpoint. The scheme allows you to put defenders in one on one matchups that you know your skill players will win. But drawing it up on paper and executing it are two different things. If you don't have the personnel to execute the spread or handle pressure, you will be one of the many spread teams that can't control the ball, turn it over, get sacked often, put pressure on their own defense, and lose by wide margins.

Outside Zone

Theme: Formation spreads field; zone blocking gives H many potential run lanes

Bubble Screen

Theme: Spread screens force D to defend width of the field; gets O speed in space

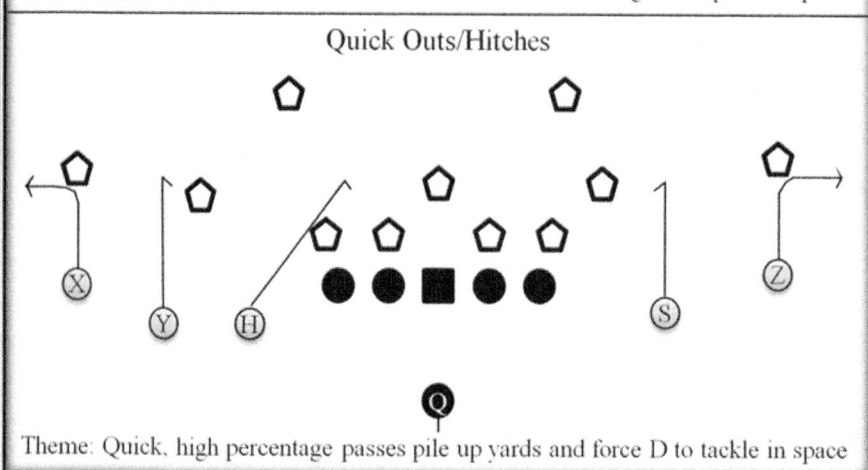

Quick Outs/Hitches

Theme: Quick, high percentage passes pile up yards and force D to tackle in space

Hurry up spread

Basic alignment:

Shotgun, spread receivers, usually at least one running back.

Brief description:

There are several variants of the hurry up spread. Some teams use wing T schemes out of the spread (Gus Malzahn). Others combine zone running with option elements (Chip Kelly/Oregon, Rich Rodriguez, etc). Others are pass first, Air Raid offenses that seek varying levels of balance in the run game (Dana Holgorsen/West Virginia, Kevin Sumlin/Texas A&M, Mike Gundy/Oklahoma State, Art Briles/Baylor, Sonny Dykes/the Tony Franklin system/Louisiana Tech/Cal, etc). The common thread among these offenses is that tempo is as important as scheme. By snapping the ball as fast as possible, the offense prevents the defense from substituting or making defensive adjustments from play to play. This leads to simplistic defensive schemes, mental breakdowns, and fatigue, in turn leading to big plays and touchdowns for the offense.

Hurry up spread offenses are usually simple, running basic run and pass plays over and over and over again. This leads to great execution. The pace of the offense, and the limitations it places on the defense, leads to simple and clear reads for the quarterback. It allows the offense to run more plays than the typical offense, spreading the ball to more skill players. The benefits extend to the practice field, where the pace of the offense means more practice repetitions, further boosting execution. To many coaches, the hurry up spread is the wave of the future.

Good for:

A well conditioned team is a must.

The quarterback needs to be a good thrower if you are to run the Air Raid variation of the hurry up spread, but if you are running the spread option variation, he can be a good athlete with a decent arm.

Teams with speed in space will thrive. Athletes who can win in space will allow the offense to take advantage of the breakdowns that the hurry up spread will cause. Size is not important.

Athletic linemen who can block in space are required.

Teams with depth at the skill positions will keep many players happy while putting extra pressure on the defense with fresh players.

If you have enough talent to execute the offense, it can help you beat more talented teams.

Bad for:

If your team is out of shape, you can't run the hurry up spread.

Your team must at least have decent talent. A subpar team running the spread will lose faster, by more points.

Slow teams should look to a different offense.

Advantages:

More repetitions in practice. An overlooked but advantageous element of the hurry up spread is the ability to run more plays in practice, especially if you have the ability to film practice and review it with your team. The pace of the offense means that you can run more plays than a typical offense, and you can do your coaching through film review. Combining the hurry up pace with the simplicity of the spread means you will get hundreds more reps of your base plays than a team that practices at a traditional pace, which should give you a comparative execution advantage.

If you practice at the proper pace, your players will be conditioned without needing to use practice time on traditional conditioning.

Will keep your skill players happy.

Gets speed in space.

Big play, quick strike, big scoring offense that is never out of a game.

Most players love this offense.

Takes advantage of athletes.

If you have enough talent to execute the basic elements of the spread, the hurry up can help you defeat teams with more talent. It forces the defense to play your game, at your pace, and you'll be well conditioned and have great mastery of your playbook.

You force the defense to align as soon as soon as the ball is placed, but you don't have to run the play immediately. You can control the clock and prevent substitutions in this way.

Drawbacks:

If you don't have the talent to execute the spread, you will give the ball back to the opposition quickly, which will put more pressure on your defense and lead to blowouts in games that you might have kept close with a traditional pace.

If you care about winning the time of possession, look elsewhere.

Because you will often lose time of possession, your defense will be on the field longer. If you care about defensive statistics, the hurry up spread is not for you.

You must fully commit. Don't try to combine the hurry up spread with a traditionally paced I formation. You'll get nothing out of either one. If you can't commit to running a simple offense with a strong identity at a sprinter's pace, you won't get the execution benefits in practice that make the offense great.

Your defense won't practice much against "traditional" offenses; therefore they may suffer when facing them.

Where it will work:

Everywhere. Whether it can work in the NFL is a current debate, but the results have been positive from the few teams that have incorporated it. Forms of the hurry up offense led the Bengals and Bills to Super Bowls in the late 80s/early 90s (although each was more complex than the modern hurry up spread). The offense is only now reemerging in the NFL.

Where it won't work:

The simple forms can be run at all levels.

Defenses that it will beat:

Poorly conditioned, undisciplined, or slow defenses will die against the hurry up spread.

Defenses that it will struggle against:

Conditioned, disciplined, and fast defenses will hurt the spread. Size is not a requirement.

Final Word:

If you choose the hurry up spread, you must fully commit. This means a strong commitment to conditioning in the offseason, developing a no huddle communication system that is easy for your players to understand but hard for your opponents to decipher, and to executing a simple offense from day one. The offense won't beat defenses by scheme or complexity; it will beat them by execution and pace. It can work at all levels of football - the plays are simple enough for youth players, while the Patriots and Tom Brady have utilized aspects of the no huddle spread to take advantage of a versatile roster and to provide Brady with easy reads. If you have a group of players who want to work hard to become the best conditioned team in your league, this offense will take advantage of their efforts. Be aware, however: if you don't have the talent or conditioning required to run the hurry up spread, you will lose by more in this offense.

Oregon Inside Zone/Read

Theme: Line counts, matches their 6 to D's 6. QB only reads if there is a 7th in box

Outside Zone/Bubble Screen (Packaged Concept)

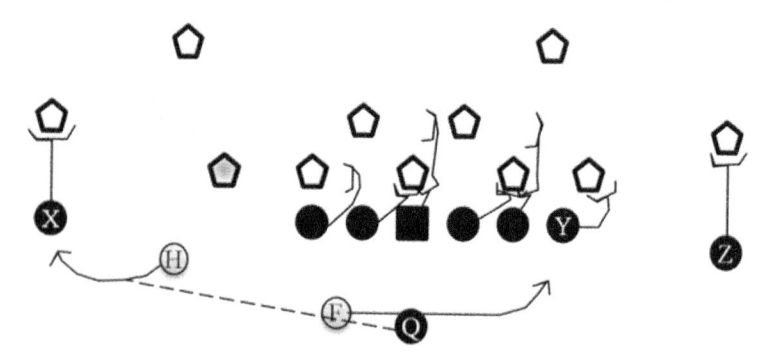

Theme: QB reads flat defender; if in box, throws bubble; if outside, hands off

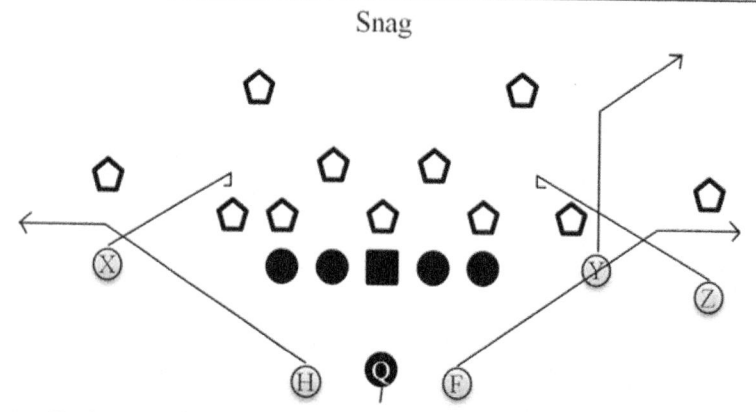

Snag

Theme: Horizontal stretch gives QB easy read on flat defenders; Y is a deep

Pistol Offense

Basic alignment:

The defining feature of the pistol offense is a quarterback 3-4 yards behind the center, with a running back 3-4 yards behind the quarterback.

Brief description:

Football coaches argue whether the pistol offense is an offense or a formation. It is both. Many teams use the pistol alignment as an additional formation in their offense. This chapter is about the pistol offense, as created and popularized by Chris Ault at the University of Nevada at Reno.

The pistol offense combines the passing benefits of the shotgun alignment with the ability to run downhill; in a normal shotgun formation, the running back is next to the quarterback, and must move horizontally before he moves vertically. The pistol lets him run straight downhill.

At its heart, the pistol offense is a power running, veer option scheme. Moving the quarterback back from under center gives him improved vision in the passing game and an extra moment to make his option reads.

Although known as a running offense, the pistol borrows from the spread and one back offenses, creating the opportunity for balance. While quarterbacking the pistol offense at Nevada, Colin Kaepernick became the only Division 1 FBS quarterback to throw for over 10,000 yards and rush for over 4,000 yards in a career. In 2009, Nevada became the first team in NCAA history to have three players rush for over 1,000 yards in the same season.

Good for:

Teams that have a fast, dynamic quarterback will take advantage of his talents in this offense. The quarterback makes his option reads 3-4 yards deep in the backfield, which means he needs to cover more ground to gain yards than in a traditional option offense.

A hard charging, downhill running back is a plus.

Because of the spread elements, the offensive line must be competent or it will be exposed.
An undersized line can function well in the pistol.

Bad for:

If you don't have a fast quarterback, you will lose some of the benefits of the pistol. He must be faster in the pistol than in traditional veer offenses, because when he makes his decision in the pistol, he is 3-4 yards deep in the backfield. He must be able to cover ground quickly.

If your offensive line can't stop penetration, negative plays will become a problem. If you have an athletic quarterback but you can't throw the ball well, defenses will be able to outnumber you in the run game.

Advantages:

The pistol is a power, big play running offense that has a more complete passing game than most option teams. The team that created it - Nevada - became a top rushing team in the NCAA, and the pistol helped them to defeat teams with superior talent and resources. It is an equalizing offense, but unlike most equalizing offenses, it is a balanced scheme that can be prolific through the air, even though it is known as a run offense.

Provides the benefits of the shotgun with a downhill running threat.

Can incorporate aspects from a wide range of offenses.

Can control the time of possession with the run or come from behind with the pass.

Drawbacks:

Nevada was most successful when it had Colin Kaepernick at quarterback. Kaepernick is one of the fastest and most dynamic quarterbacks to ever play college football. Other teams have struggled after installing the pistol as a base offense (such as UCLA). The sample size is small, but one must wonder if a Kaepernick-esque quarterback is a requirement to make the offense excel.

If you don't have a line that can prevent penetration, you'll suffer negative plays because the quarterback/running back mesh occurs deeper in the backfield. If you want to compensate for a weak line by running the option, consider more traditional option offenses such as the split t, veer, wishbone, or flexbone.

Where it will work:

The pistol formation can be incorporated at all levels. The pistol offense is best suited for college, high school, and youth teams, although the Washington Redskins have used aspects of the pistol offense to great success with Robert Griffin III. Griffin – like Kaepernick – is one of the most athletic quarterbacks the game has ever seen.

Where it won't work:

The pistol can work at all levels. While an NFL team will never run the pistol exclusively, the Redskins have shown with Griffin (as have the 49ers with Kaepernick, to a lesser extent) that the pistol veer can work as a base scheme in the NFL. The pistol formation will continue as a staple at all levels due to the downhill running/shotgun passing combination.

Defenses that it will beat:

Undisciplined defenses struggle against the option.

Defenses that aren't stout at the point of attack will have trouble with the downhill running game.

Defenses that it will struggle against:

Stout, disciplined, fast defenses will give the pistol trouble. They'll give every offense trouble.

Final Word:

The pistol offense is the latest high scoring iteration of the option. Nevada took its program to new heights with the pistol, and other programs were quick to jump on the bandwagon. None of them have achieved the same success as Nevada. Like other option offenses, the pistol requires commitment over years, not months. The personnel must match the scheme, and the most important piece - a dynamic quarterback - is also one of the hardest players to find in football. A coach must be committed to the pistol in the long run, and must have the talent to incorporate it. If he does, he'll be rewarded with a grinding, big play rushing attack and balanced pass game that will keep his defense off the field and win games.

Pistol Inside Veer

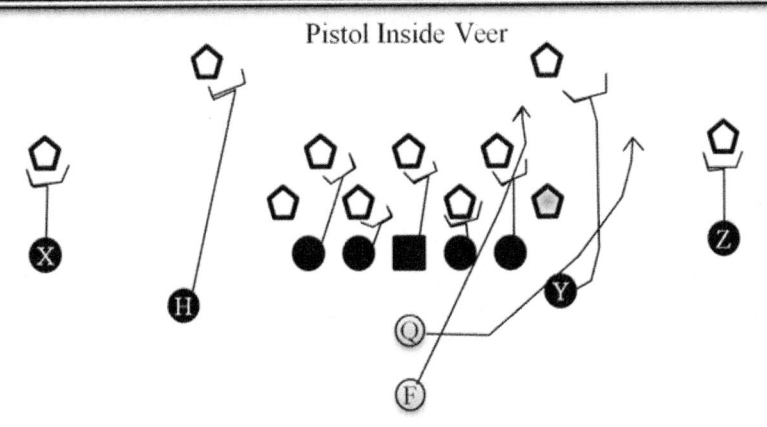

Theme: QB reads 1st DL on/outside T, allowing inside wall and blocks downfield

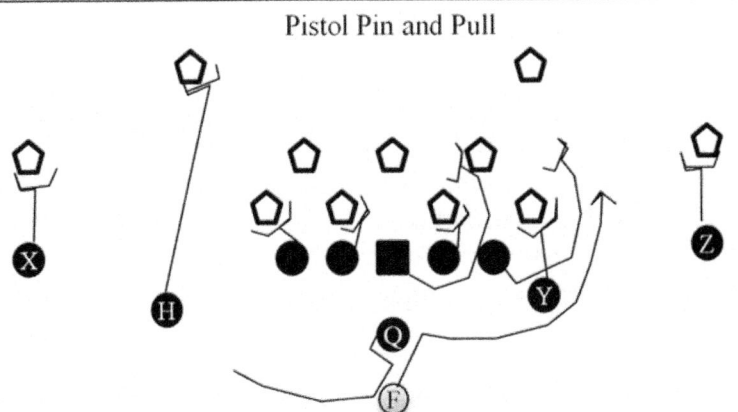

Pistol Pin and Pull

Theme: RB influences inside then bounces while OL pin men on/inside or pull

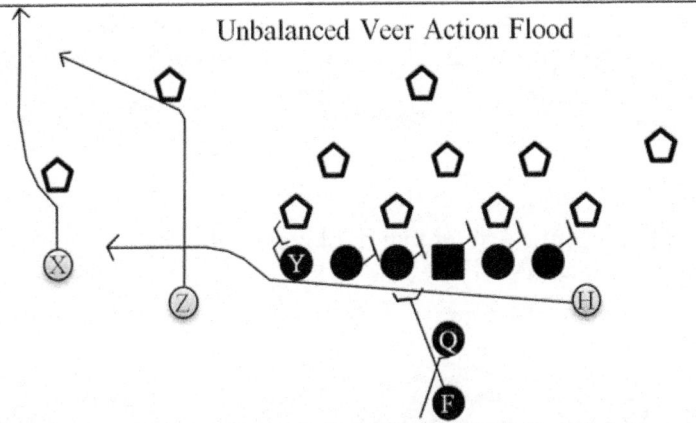

Unbalanced Veer Action Flood

Theme: Play action with wing slip behind OL, half field read & 7 man protection

Multiple

Basic alignment:

Varied.

Brief description:

A multiple offense borrows elements from many offensive systems. It usually has a versatile play calling language that allows the coach to adjust play and formation without limit. The goal is for run/pass balance and the ability to adjust to any defense. The coach can tailor the offense for each opponent during a week of practice or on the fly during the game. The players are accustomed to adjusting base plays to various formations, giving the offense great versatility. This versatility often comes at the expense of execution, and multiple offenses can struggle to establish an identity. Once a staple at all levels of football, the multiple offense has gone out of favor in recent years, as coaches have reverted to less versatile "system" offenses in order to execute better.

Good for:

Teams with good talent and players who are both physically and mentally capable of digesting and executing schemes from various systems. A good throwing quarterback is a necessity to achieve balance.

Bad for:

If you don't have good talent and players who can adjust to and execute the various schemes, you will have a mishmash of poorly executed plays from various offenses. Stick to a "system" offense instead.

If you don't have a capable throwing quarterback, you can't achieve the balance at the heart of a good multiple offense.

Advantages:

Tailor your offense to any opponent. When a multiple offense is rolling, it confuses the defense with multiple formations and run/pass schemes, and attacks the vulnerabilities of each defense.

You can achieve balance, and win with either the run or the pass. You are never out of the game because of your ability to pass, and you can salt away a victory with your running game.

Drawbacks:

Unless you have the talent (both on the field and in your coaching staff) to teach and execute the system, execution will suffer and you will have little identity.

Lengthy play calls can lead to confusion and missed assignments. Players may be unsure of assignments and play slow.

Playbooks are long and complex. Learning can be difficult for players.

If you try to execute a little bit of everything, you may end up executing nothing.

Where it will work:

All levels, although it is unlikely to succeed at the youth level. A multiple offense is best suited for the NFL.

Where it won't work:

Most young kids can't remember the plays in a true multiple offense.

Defenses that it will beat:

Any defense; versatility is the benefit of the multiple offense.

Defenses that it will struggle against:

Any defense; lack of execution is the drawback of the multiple offense.

Final Word:

When multiple offenses are rolling, they are nearly unstoppable. Each defense is dissected, and plays are run to exploit every weakness and matchup advantage. This is a great offense for the "mad genius coach" who loves drawing up new plays each week. It can take advantage of all of your players, and defeat any defense. But a coach walks a fine line with a multiple offense. Make sure that you establish an identity, and stick with it. If you don't - or if you add too many plays and tinker too often - your team will be good at nothing. You may have a few good weeks, but your performance will be inconsistent, based more upon the success of your weekly game plan than on consistent execution. An offense won't work as a collection of random plays. Make sure that your team can execute what you install if you want to run a multiple offense.

Outside Zone

Theme: Versatile play known for cutbacks as OL doubles DL and moves to LBs

Bunch Curl/Post with backside option route

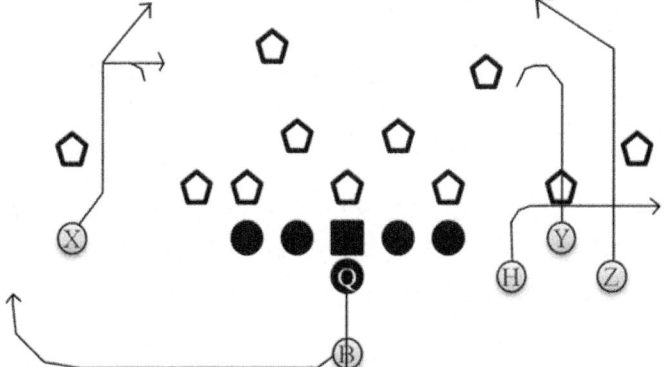

Theme: If safety jumps the curl, post can hit big over the top

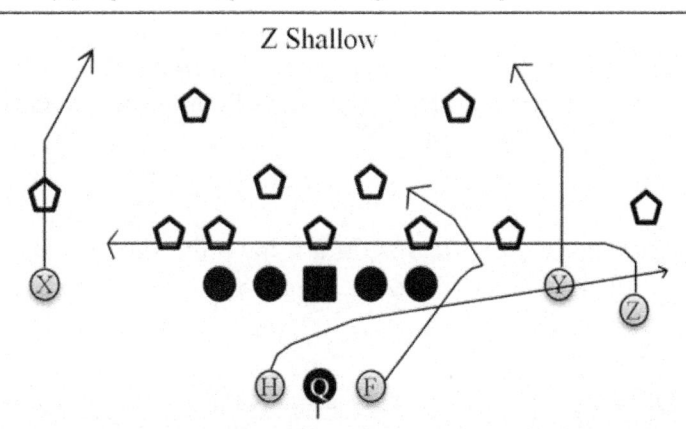

Z Shallow

Theme: X and Y push coverage deep while Z and F force great LB communication

"Matchup" Offense

Basic alignment:

Varied.

Brief description:

The "matchup" offense is not an offense per se. No team says that they run a "matchup" offense. However, many teams change their schemes and plays each week after scouting their opponent. The theory is that they will use plays to attack the weaknesses in personnel and scheme of each opponent. Such an offense usually incorporates basic running and passing schemes, but augments them each week with new formations and plays. It is an extreme version of the multiple offense, more predicated on scouting and creating individual plays than on incorporating various schemes.

This does not refer to an offense that scouts a defense and creates a few plays each week to beat it. It refers to an offense that has no identity besides having no identity; that is, an offense that drastically changes its playbook each week for each opponent.

Good for:

Professional and some college teams who have the time and players who can implement and execute new schemes on a weekly basis.

Bad for:

Everyone else. Most teams do not have the time or personnel to be able to change their playbook week by week without a significant drop in execution.

Advantages:

Allows an offense to tailor their game plan to defeat the weaknesses of each opponent. This can result in big plays and the ability to exploit schematic and personnel weaknesses of each defense.

Drawbacks:

A "matchup" approach will kill execution for most teams.

Where it will work:

The NFL and some major college programs.

Where it won't work:

Everywhere else.

Defenses that it will beat:

The matchup approach is more successful against defenses that blitz heavily, play man-to-man defense, or that do not have a well rounded approach to defense. A good coach in a matchup offense will design plays to attack schematic vulnerabilities and garner favorable matchups.

Defenses that it will struggle against:

Disciplined, conservative defenses that are rarely caught out of position or susceptible to big plays will be harder to exploit schematically.

Final Word:

Using a "matchup" approach to offense is not recommended outside of the NFL or some major college programs (and it should be used with great caution at those levels). Those teams can use such an approach and have a chance for success because the players are good enough to learn and execute new schemes with regularity.

Becoming a matchup team is tempting, because it allows you to draw up the perfect plays for any opponent. But your offense is only as good as the plays that it can execute. If you change your philosophy each week, you will rarely execute well enough to win. Just because teams in the NFL can execute huge playbooks doesn't mean that other teams can. NFL athletes are professionals who have the time and ability to execute such an offense. For the vast majority of coaches, a better approach is to find a philosophy, stick to it, execute it, and make small adjustments to combat individual opponents.

Wham

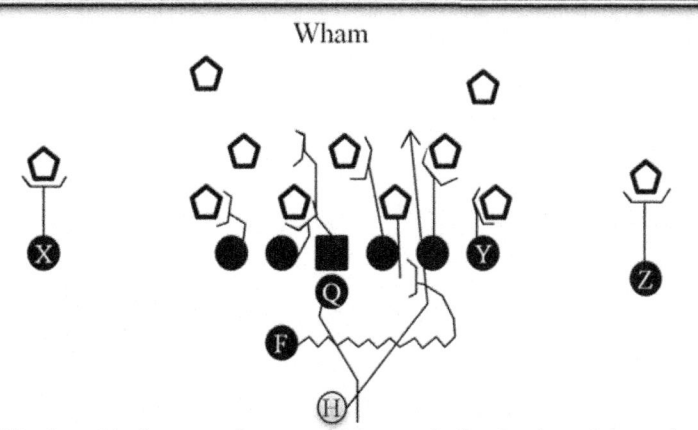

Theme: FB wham block comes from surprising angle for dominant/aggressive DT

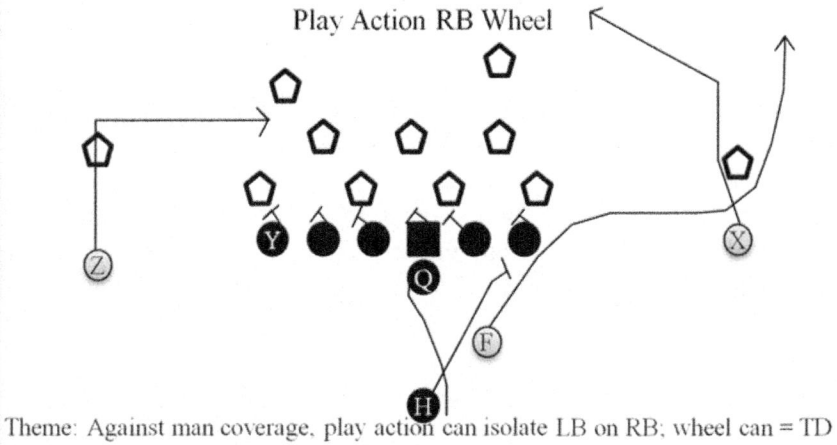

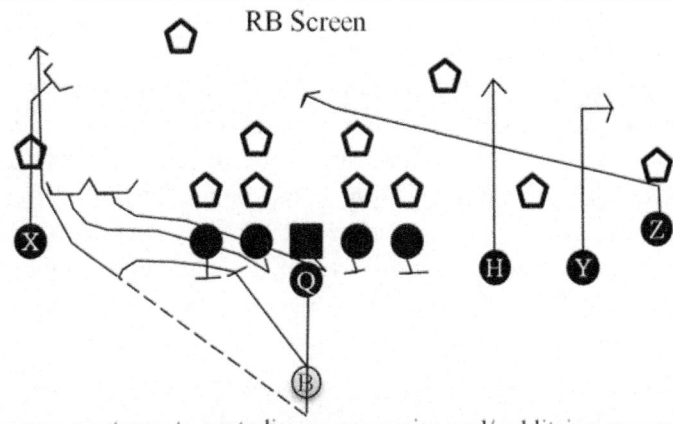

Play Action RB Wheel

Theme: Against man coverage, play action can isolate LB on RB; wheel can = TD

RB Screen

Theme: Screens a great way to neutralize an aggressive and/or blitzing pass rush

"Pro" Offense

Basic alignment:

Varied.

Brief description:

When people talk about a "pro" offense, they are talking about one that is balanced, varied, and vast. A pro offense has staple plays and schemes that give it an identity, but also borrows from other schemes and installs new plays for individual opponents. Game plans change weekly. Although traditional aspects of the pro offense are drop back passing and a two back running game, the line between college and pro offenses has blurred with the adoption of spread, no huddle, and read option elements to the pro game.

High schools and youth teams can run a pared down version of the pro offense, which is a balanced approach with a two back run game and drop back passing game.

Good for:

Teams that have good talent, a prototypical quarterback, and players who can learn a large playbook can run a true pro offense.

Of course, the offense is good for professional teams. Simplified versions are also good for talented teams at lower levels. It allows them to outplay competition with a balanced, well rounded attack, as opposed to a "system" offense that is not balanced and/or is more predicated on execution. The balance and ability to adjust in a pro offense allows a powerhouse team to beat any opponent, regardless of that opponent's strengths, whereas a more rigid "system" offense may struggle against a team that is well constructed to stop their scheme.

Bad for:

Teams that don't have a good quarterback cannot run a competent pro passing game.

If you have a talent disadvantage, a pro offense won't help you to overcome it like a "system" offense would.

If your players have trouble learning plays, the pro offense is not for you.

Advantages:

The most balanced of offenses, the pro attack is designed to run, pass, and take advantage of skill players at all positions. You can win games on the ground or through the air. If a defense is strong against the run, a pro attack can beat it with the pass. If a defense is strong against the pass, a pro attack can beat it with the run. Because of this balance, it is a good choice for teams with good or superior talent who don't want to get caught by an underdog who does one thing well.

Drawbacks:

The only teams that can incorporate the volume of plays in a true professional playbook and maintain execution are professional teams and a select few college teams.

It is harder to establish an identity with such a balanced offense, particularly if an amateur team tries to run more plays than the players can execute.

Where it will work:

The NFL, and a select few major colleges. The balanced form can work at all levels.

Where it won't work:

In its most expansive form, it won't work for most teams below the NFL level.

Defenses that it will beat:

If a pro offense has superior personnel or a superior game plan, it can beat any defense.

Defenses that it will struggle against:

Any defense that can match up physically can play against a pro offense.

Final Word:

There is no singular pro offense. While each NFL offense does have an identity (for example, zone blocking, or more spread oriented, or more two back oriented, etc), they also borrow from everywhere, and overhaul their game plans for each opponent. While teams at every level can and should game plan, few can incorporate as many schemes and techniques as the pros. For most teams, you are better off with a stripped down version of the pro offense - five or six run plays, five or six passing concepts, a few specials and a few weekly plays. This will give you the balance you desire with the execution you need. You'll have a complete offense with all the runs, passes, screens and trick plays needed to beat any opponent. The pros are the pros for a reason - they are paid millions of dollars to focus their lives on studying and learning and adapting on a weekly basis. Keeping it simple is better for the vast majority of teams.

Counter Trey

Theme: Back action to left influences LBs while guard and tackle pull to the right

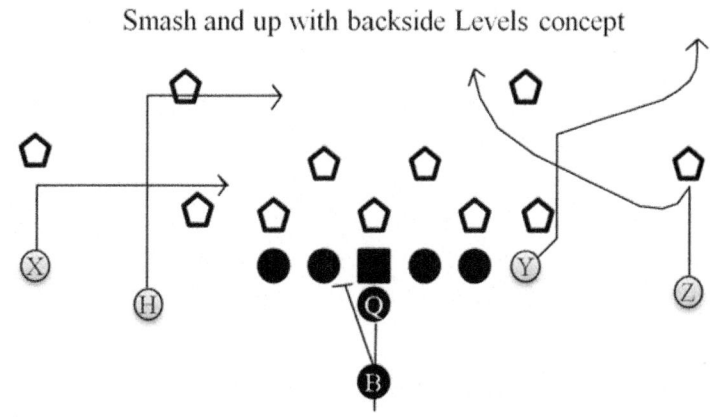

Smash and up with backside Levels concept

Theme: Anticipates C2 Smash D, which leaves void between safeties and TE on S

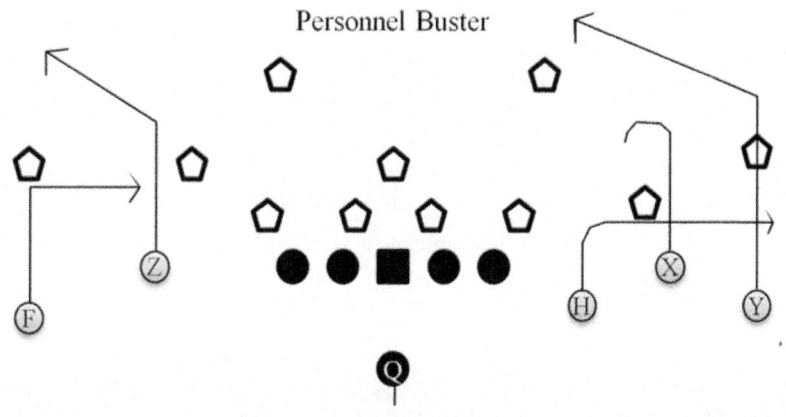

Personnel Buster

Theme: TE, FB, HB tells defense run; versatility of NFL players allows spread

Printed in Great Britain
by Amazon